YOU CAN BE A PUPPETEER!

YOU CAN BE A PUPPETEER!

A Complete "How-to" Book on Puppets and Plays

by
CAROLYN LONDON

Member of
THE PUPPETEERS OF AMERICA

MOODY PRESS
CHICAGO

© 1972 by
THE MOODY BIBLE INSTITUTE
OF CHICAGO

ISBN: 0-8024-9824-8

Third Printing, 1974

Printed in the United States of America

To Paul

Contents

CHAPTER	PAGE
Introduction to Puppetry	9

Part I—PUPPETS

1.	Sack Puppets	17
2.	Talking Puppets	24
3.	Hand Puppets	31
4.	How to Make Your Puppet Come Alive	47

Part II—PLAYS

5.	The Play	59
6.	Broken Windshield	62
7.	Baby Moses	71
8.	Elisha and the Widow's Oil	82
9.	Idol Breaker	88
10.	Pinata	97
11.	Wong Lee's Mystery Box	108
12.	Dorcas Raised from the Dead	115

Introduction to Puppetry

You can become a puppeteer. With only a few hours of enjoyable work, and with very little cash outlay, you can develop an exciting method of presenting the story of the Lord Jesus Christ and His work around the world.

The history of puppetry is a long and glorious one. Puppets were used thousands of years ago in China and India. Aristotle, in the fourth century B.C. likens the lord of all creation to a puppeteer who merely pulls the strings to act out his will.

The early church used puppetry to present the Nativity scene and other Bible stories. But perhaps no generation of children has been more exposed to puppets than the present one. Besides TV, puppets are used in schools, and more recently have begun to be used again in the churches.

Children like to see things. A play acted out by puppets will impress on their minds the message that the teacher wants to get across.

Leslie Stobbe, editor of Moody Press, says that the hand puppet is one of the more exciting visual tools a teacher can use.

Puppetry and puppet plays are not limited to children. Adults and teenagers as well, are fascinated by their exciting presentations.

There are several different basic types of puppets.

1. The glove or hand—sometimes called fist—puppet, that is controlled by the performer's hand inside the puppet.

2. Rod puppet that is controlled by rods. One rod supports the puppet and one or two other rods move the puppet's head and arms. These rod puppets require both hands, and sometimes two performers. They are extensively used in Java and other parts of the Orient.
3. Shadow puppets that are usually flat cut-out figures. These are held behind a curtain and lit from the rear so that the audience sees only the puppets' shadows. This type of puppetry has not gained much acceptance in the United States, although it is widely used in the Orient.
4. Marionettes that are complete puppets, with movable arms, legs, and heads. They are much more versatile than the hand puppets, but they are much more difficult to make and handle, and they require years of hard practice to control. They are operated by strings held from above the stage.

There are variations of these puppets; sometimes a combination of the two kinds, for example, a hand and rod puppet, may be used. This is a puppet whose head is controlled from inside by the performer's hand, and whose arms are controlled by the performer's other hand by means of rods.

This book is not designed for the professional puppeteer who has hours to spend designing and making his puppets and learning how to control them. It is for the very busy Sunday school or Bible school teacher who wants to learn a new and effective way of presenting the old truths of the Bible. The hand puppet answers this need with the least effort and expenditure of time, and with great effectiveness.

Almost anything can be turned into a hand puppet. Take a handkerchief, drape it over one hand (fig. *a*). Now, holding the cloth securely with the ring finger and little finger, bring your thumb and middle finger forward (figs. *b* and *c*). You now have an old woman. To bring her to life, bend your index finger forward slightly, so that your old woman is hunched over, her shoulders bent with years of hardship. Now make

Introduction to Puppetry

your hand move very slowly forward, and as you do, turn it slightly from side to side and very slightly up and down at the same time (fig. *d*). You make four movements at once, but they are not hard to do.

When you have mastered this, you have mastered the most important movement of the hand puppet—walking. Now, placing your arm below the level of the tabletop, and letting only your covered hand show above the table, move your old woman slowly forward. Be sure that your whole arm moves. Do not keep your elbow in one place, or your old woman will soon fall on her face and disappear into the "ground" (fig. *e*). Make your elbow move at the same time your hand moves (fig. *f*). Your old woman is now alive. She walks! She's a tired old woman, and her body is bowed, not only by the weight of her years, but by the burden on her heart.

You see, she's never heard that the Lord Jesus loves her. All her life she's tried to do the things that were right, but now, she is certain that her work has been in vain. She knows that her sins are still with her. Perhaps she's an old woman from a foreign country. She's tried sacrifices and offerings to the gods of her tribe, but these haven't brought her peace or happiness.

Do you see how your old woman has now developed a personality? But you mustn't leave her there. Ask the children what should be done for this old woman. Get your audience involved with her so that they want to help solve her plight.

Oh, yes, someone should go and tell the old woman about the Lord Jesus. That someone who tells about the Lord Jesus is a missionary. Who can be a missionary? Yes, all who believe in Jesus can and should be missionaries. Some can go across the ocean, others must be missionaries here at home.

So make a missionary out of your other hand. Hold up your index finger. Put a "hat" on the missionary's head. (This can be an eraser or a rubber finger protector or a glob of plasticine or clay, or a ribbon—anything to suggest a hat.) You can have a colored handkerchief over the finger, under the hat or you can use a bare finger. Now make your missionary move toward the old woman. The walking procedure is the same as for the old woman, but this missionary stands tall and straight. The missionary moves close to the old woman and says, "Friend, I have left my country to tell you about the Lord Jesus."

Ask the children what the missionary should do for the old woman. Is she sick? What should the missionary say? How can she help the old woman? As the problem is resolved, move the two characters off the stage together.

You have just created two characters with real personalities. For a few minutes you, as well as your class, have looked at your fingers, not as part of your hand, but as people with real problems and real solutions. You have brought life to your hands, to your puppets. You have learned how to make them walk, and you have learned that their posture has identified them—one as old, one as young and strong.

These finger puppets and variations of them, are suitable for small classes and younger children, but they are not good for larger audiences. For these you need slightly larger puppets so that they will be easily seen.

Your ability to present puppet plays does not depend on any natural talent. You do not have to be an artist to create believable puppets, nor do you have to be a playwright to produce suitable material for your puppet characters. But you do have to follow a few basic rules. By learning these principles, the hand puppeteer can make his puppets come alive. You make your puppet live. In your hands he can walk, run, kick, laugh, cry, fall asleep, hit someone, or caress someone; he can be arrogant, humble, afraid, courageous, weak, or strong. You give him the personality that will present the message you want your audience to hear and understand. Unlike most TV puppets, your puppets are not primarily for entertainment. They

Introduction to Puppetry 13

are to instruct in the most vital thing your children will ever know—how to believe in the Lord Jesus Christ and obey His commandments.

Figs. *a-d.* A simple handkerchief puppet

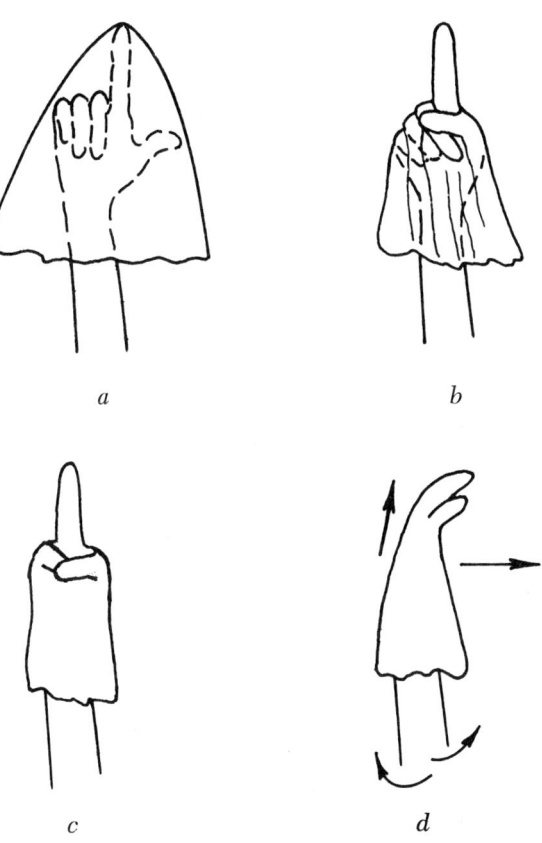

Figs. *e-f*. Walking the puppet

e Wrong

f Right

Part I

PUPPETS

1

Sack Puppets

Of all the puppets used in modern Sunday schools and Bible classes, the paper bag puppet is the best known and easiest to make. This puppet, used in the proper way, is appropriate for any age, but it has its best usage with the four to seven year olds.

The paper bag can be used in one of two ways:

1. Empty, but with a face drawn on it. The hand of the performer makes all the movements.
2. Stuffed, with paper towels or newspapers. This puppet has less mobility than the empty sack.

The empty paper sack can either have the mouth or the eyes move. If your puppet is going to do a lot of "talking" it should be made so that the mouth can move (fig. 1a). If the eyes of your puppet are to do a lot of work, then the eyes can be drawn on the flap so that they appear to open or close (fig. 1b).

"Hair" can be applied to the sack puppet with Scotch tape or glue. This can be a dish mop, ruffled crepe paper, an old wig, or it can be drawn on with crayon or poster paint. You can paint or glue teeth, ears, earrings, beads, or eyeglasses onto your sack puppets to make them fit the personalities they are supposed to represent. They are easily manipulated by putting your fingers inside the flap so that the tips are on the bottom of the fold. The features may be painted on, but they are more interesting if they are made out of bits of fur, felt, cotton, feathers, or other heavily textured materials, and then glued onto the sack.

Animal puppets are made by applying ears, or a mane, or whiskers (fig. 1c).

"Sad Sack" (fig. 1d) has tears made out of clear glass beads, or thick blobs of white or colorless glue.

The puppet "Nightmare" is made by folding the bottom of the sack at the middle. (See fig. 1e.) Paint the inside of the fold red, and apply large "horse teeth" but cutting them out of heavy white paper. Then draw the rest of the mouth and the eyes, and fasten on ears made of heavy paper.

The stuffed paper sack puppets can be made so that the head will move, but not the eyes. By being very careful to crease the sack in the proper place and hold it firmly with your fingers, you can make a movable mouth.

To make a movable head, stuff the paper sack loosely with crumpled newspaper or paper towels. (Paper toweling is preferred as it is more flexible.) Paint on the features that you wish, or glue them and add whatever adornment is needed. A king wears a crown; old people have gray hair, made out of absorbent cotton or a white dust mop; a young girl might have yarn braids (figs. 1f and 1g). Now, near the top of the sack (bottom of the puppet), tie a string loosely to hold the stuffing in. You must be able to insert your hand easily. Move your hand in the stuffing so that you have a comfortable place to work, but remember that the stuffing must be firm enough to allow you to move your puppet easily. You must be able to move the head up and down or to the right or left.

A movable-mouth puppet is done in the same way as the stuffed paper sack above, except the mouth is not added until you have inserted your hand. At the place you want the mouth

Sack Puppets

to be, grasp a piece of the paper sack with your fingers that are inside the sack (fig. 1g). With your free hand, push the paper sack gently between the thumb and index finger of the hand inside the puppet. Now crease this firmly. Withdraw your hand and paint the mouth around this crease, and glue on the teeth, if desired. The inside of the crease can be painted red to enhance the illusion of a mouth. When you insert your hand to perform, be sure that you catch this crease again between the thumb and index finger. The puppet is made to "talk" by moving the thumb and index fingers.

Paper sack puppets are somewhat limited in their use, because they are essentially comic puppets. They can be used for teaching memory verses or songs, or for making special announcements of coming events. Because the puppet has limited motion, the announcements and the puppet plays should be kept short to hold the child's attention.

As the talking puppet's mouth can move, or the eye puppet's eyes move, there is very little difficulty in creating the illusion that the puppet is actually talking. However, only one puppet at a time should be moving, unless the other's movements are essential to the point of the story. If both puppets are to say something at the same time, then of course, there must be two performers. With sack puppets, as with other types of hand puppets, the suggestion that the puppet is talking must come from the movement of the puppet. That is the reason that it is essential to keep the other puppet quiet while the first is "talking."

When putting on short skits, the teacher should coach the children so that they are familiar with the dialogue, but not try to make them memorize the lines. If the skit is to be about a coming event, the only things that need to be memorized would be the time and place.

Here are a couple suggestions for skits, using paper sack puppets and children for performers.

VBS

CHARACTERS: Eye (moving eye sack puppet)
Mouth (talking sack puppet)

(These can be made to represent either two boys, two girls, or a boy and a girl.)

(*Scene opens with* EYE *asleep.*)

MOUTH (*enters*): I have just heard the very best news! I'm so excited.

EYE (*opens eyes*): Go away, I'm sleepy. I don't want to be bothered. It's vacation time.

MOUTH: I know! That's what's so exciting.

EYE (*closes eyes*): What's so exciting about vacation? Nothing to do. I'm going to sleep all summer.

MOUTH: Well, you can sleep if you want to, but you'll be sorry.

EYE: You'll be sorry if you don't go away.

MOUTH: I'm going someplace exciting—I'm going to—

EYE (*opens eyes*): I don't want to hear it. (*Closes eyes.*)

MOUTH: You'll be sorry. I'm going to have fun. We're going to hear exciting stories, there's going to be special speakers, and I'm going to learn a lot of new things. In fact, I'm going to learn to make puppets just like us.

EYE (*opens eyes*): You're going to make WHAT?

MOUTH: Puppets.

EYE: I'm people, not puppets.

MOUTH: You're a puppet.

EYE: You talk too much. I'm sleepy. (*closes eyes*) Go 'way. (*Opens eyes*) Where is this place you're going to go?

MOUTH: It's Vacation Bible School. It starts tomorrow, right here in this building—at nine in the morning.

EYE (*closes eyes*): Too early. I'm going to sleep.

MOUTH: It'll be lots of fun. We'll sing songs, and make things—

EYE (*opens eyes*): Am I a puppet? I thought I was people.

MOUTH: Come to Vacation Bible School and find out.

Sack Puppets

Eye: When is this Vacation Bible School?
Mouth: Tomorrow at nine. Everybody's welcome.
Eye (*closes eyes*): I think I'll come. Wake me up so I can get to Vacation Bible School on time. I want to find out if I'm people or puppets.
Mouth (*to audience*): And everyone of you, be sure to come to Vacation Bible School tomorrow. It's going to be fun!

Picnic

Characters: Nightmare (talking sack puppet)
Sad Sack (moving eye sack puppet)

(*Open* Nightmare's *mouth each time he speaks. Open and close* Sad Sack's *eyes each time he speaks.*)

Sad Sack: Oh, boohoo! Boohoo! BOOHOO!
Nightmare (*whinnies*): Neigh! Don't cry, Sad Sack. Why are you sad?
Sad Sack: Oh, Nightmare, I'm sorry to see you.
Nightmare: I thought you'd be glad.
Sad Sack: I missed the Sunday school picnic, you know.
Nightmare: I thought you said you wanted to go.
Sad Sack: But I forgot it, or something. I'll cry all night.
Nightmare: Wait a minute—things'll be right.
Sad Sack: Oh, boohoo, boohoo, boohoo-hoo-hoo!
Nightmare: You've no cause to cry, I want to tell you.
Sad Sack: But I missed the picnic and that's why I'm sad.
Nightmare: And now I've got news that'll make your face glad.
Sad Sack: You speak words of cheer, and this I must hear. Tell me, friend Nightmare, the words true and dear.
Nightmare: My friend, you're asleep, the picnic's next week. Wake up, my dear Sad Sack, and on next Saturday, the Sunday school picnic, with food, games, and play at (name of place) will brighten your day!
Sad Sack: You mean I'm asleep, I dreamed all this? The Sunday school picnic I didn't miss?

22 *You Can Be a Puppeteer!*

Nightmare and Sad Sack (*together*): And you, boys and girls, don't forget the great day—The picnic is special, with lots of good play.

Fig. 1*a*. Moving mouth

Fig. 1*b*. Moving eyes

Fig. 1*c*. Lion

Fig. 1*d*. Sad Sack

Sack Puppets

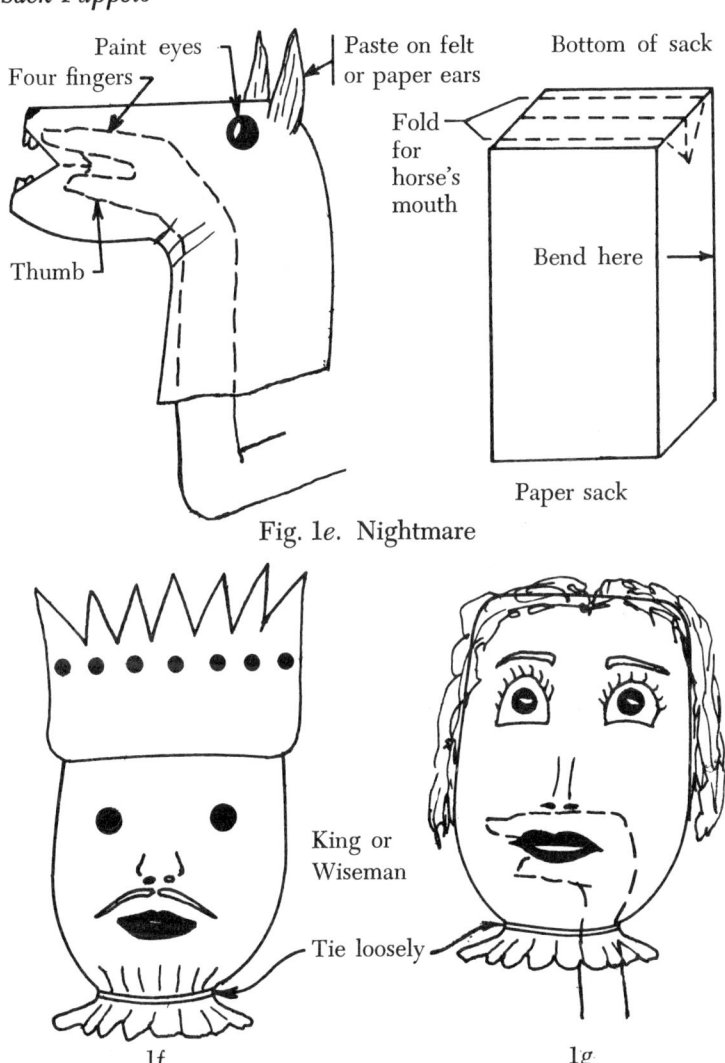

Fig. 1e. Nightmare

Figs. 1f-1g. Stuffed sack puppets

2

Talking Puppets

You have all seen these very clever talking puppets on TV. Many of them are quite elaborate and are obviously done by professional doll and puppet makers. The average Sunday school teacher has neither the time nor the equipment to make elaborate puppets like these; however, a very satisfactory and appealing moving-mouth puppet may be made in an hour or two using the material that every home has on hand, old socks and old towels.

In schools or on TV, these comedy puppets are effective as entertainers and educators, but they do have a useful role in presenting part of the Sunday school or Bible school program also. They are especially valuable in the Vacation Bible School or in the weekday Bible class where the atmosphere is less formal.

As with the paper-sack puppets, these moving-mouth or talking puppets can be used to teach memory verses, make announcements about coming events, or to help the children learn new songs. They can also be used in short skits.

Care must be taken, though, not to make the song or the Bible verse sound ridiculous in the mouth of a comic puppet. Humor, however, has a very important role to play in teaching.

The children in your Bible classes will be interested in using the puppets themselves. You might choose a different pupil each week to present the memory verse by means of the puppet.

Talking Puppets

How to Make the Sock Puppet

Although we call it a "sock" puppet, the sleeve of an old sweater will work just as well. The sock has one advantage, the heel makes a natural "head" for animal puppets. If the sock has an elasticized top, stretch it, and then gently cut the elastic threads so that the sock will slip easily over your hand. Now cut the sock, beginning at the middle of the toe, to form a mouth (fig. 2a). If you are making a cat, dog, whale, snake, etc., cut back about two inches. If you are making an alligator, cut back as far as the base of your fingers (fig. 2b).

Take an oblong of red cloth, fold it, and sew the ends to fit the shape of the toe of the sock (fig. 2c). Now sew the rest of the red insert into fit the rest of the cut (fig. 2d). Cut a half oblong of darker red cloth and sew the tongue in. Teeth may be added if desired by sewing stiff felt or cardboard at the desired places (fig. 2e). Make eyes out of large white buttons using black button thread or any bright pieces of foil or colored cloth you desire.

Whiskers, eyebrows, etc., can be made out of pipe cleaners, or heavy button thread stiffened with fingernail polish.

You now have the basis for a talking puppet, but he needs some padding to make him move in a lifelike manner. If you have some foam rubber from an old pillow (solid piece, not chips), you can use this. It is possible to stuff it with soft rags, but the foam rubber is easier to use. You need two pieces cut to the approximate width and length of the puppet's entire head. It is not necessary to be too accurate, as the soft foam rubber and the equally stretchable sock will adapt to each other. Cut two longish oblongs, one for the upper jaw and one for the lower (fig. 2f). Stuff the foam rubber into the upper jaw and work your fingers around until it is comfortable to manage the movement of the jaw. Now insert the other piece of foam rubber into the lower jaw. It will probably be necessary to take a few blind stitches in several places to hold this in

You Can Be a Puppeteer!

Actually you now have rubber-lined pockets for your four fingers and for your thumb. The thickness of the rubber padding depends on what you are making. A dog, cat, bear, or similar animal will require much thicker padding in the top part than a snake or crocodile will.

You can easily change your character by changing the eyes and the thickness of the padding. You can add wings, antennae, whiskers, eyebrows, stripes, dots, and so on, to change characters.

To make the puppet talk, insert your four fingers in the top pocket and your thumb in the bottom. Now practice in front of the mirror making the puppet's mouth move in time to the syllables in the words. This is fairly easy, but you must be careful not to make it move more or less than the words call for. As you cannot form round *O*'s with your puppet's mouth, you must move the mouth from a partly opened position to wide to simulate the forming of vowels.

This talking puppet can be made out of Turkish toweling, velvet, plush, or any knit material.

There are two Bible stories that lend themselves well to the use of talking animal puppets. One is Balaam's ass, and the other is Jonah and the great fish.

Here is a short skit using two talking animal puppets.

The Fish That Swallowed Jonah

CHARACTERS: Great Fish (much larger than the second fish)
Sardy (a small fish)

BACKGROUND: *Blue to suggest water, perhaps with a few seaweed drawn in* (fig. 2g)

SARDY: Greetings, Great Fish! How are you? The last time I saw you we were swimming peacefully around the waters at Gilbraltar, and all of a sudden, you just turned and swam off rapidly. What happened?

Talking Puppets

GREAT FISH: The strangest thing. Suddenly I felt that I had to do something very important. I swam east until I was very near the eastern coast of the Mediterranean. I knew that there was a great and important work for me to do, and I wanted to be where I could do it. I didn't know what it was.

SARDY: Wow! You make my fins stand up! There was something very important for you to do? Tell me what it was.

GREAT FISH: When I got to the place where I knew I was supposed to go, there was a terrible storm, the worst storm I've ever seen. There were all sorts of things floating around in the water, big logs, heavy barrels, boxes of all kinds. I took one look and started for deep waters where it would be quiet. But the strangest thing happened— (*Pauses.*)

SARDY: Yes, yes, go on—what?

GREAT FISH: When I got way down deep, it seemed that something, or Someone, was pushing me up—up—up—up to the top of the water.

SARDY: Yes, yes. Tell me. What was it?

GREAT FISH: There was a big ship tossing in the water, and I could hear someone shouting, "We beseech thee, O Lord, let us not perish for this man's life.' Then, then I saw him.

SARDY: Saw him? Who?

GREAT FISH: A man. The other men on the ship lifted him up in the air, and—and suddenly they threw the man overboard. I dashed down to where he was, and there was seaweed all over his head—and I opened my mouth—and he slid right down my throat.

SARDY: Then what happened?

GREAT FISH: Then, all of a sudden the wind stopped, and the sea became very calm. And I could hear the men on the ship saying that the great God of the Hebrews was the only true God. And they promised to obey this great God.

SARDY: It is too bad that people everywhere don't obey the great God of the Hebrews, our Creator God.

GREAT FISH: Well, I knew that God, the Creator God, had a plan for this man inside of me, and that I was part of that plan. The man started talking to God, and I heard him promise God that he would obey Him.

SARDY: It's too bad that he had to be in such trouble before he learned to obey God.

GREAT FISH: This man, this man inside me, he told God he'd go and preach to the people of Nineveh.

SARDY: Who are they?

GREAT FISH: They were his enemies, but God wanted them to repent and follow Him.

SARDY: So what happened then?

GREAT FISH: Well, I started swimming for the coast, and this man was inside me, and it took me three days to get there. When we got to the shore I gave one big burp, and Jonah—that was his name—landed right on the dry ground. The last I saw him he was headed for Nineveh. I sure was glad to get rid of him; he gave me a tummy ache.

SARDY: He'd have saved himself a lot of trouble if he'd done what God wanted him to do in the first place.

GREAT FISH: That's a good lesson for all of us to learn. I'm glad I could help him do what God wanted him to do, though. Well, I've got to go now. Good-bye.

SARDY: And I've got to get back to my class in school. Bye.

Talking Puppets

Figs. 2a-2f. Talking puppet

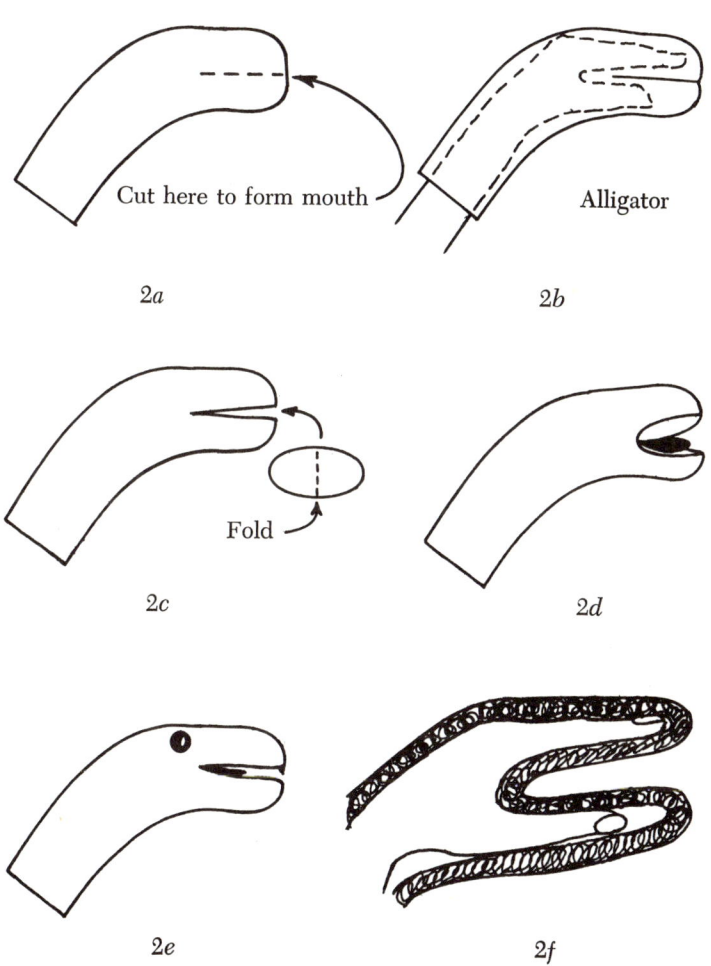

30 *You Can Be a Puppeteer!*

Fig. 2g. Great Fish and Sardy

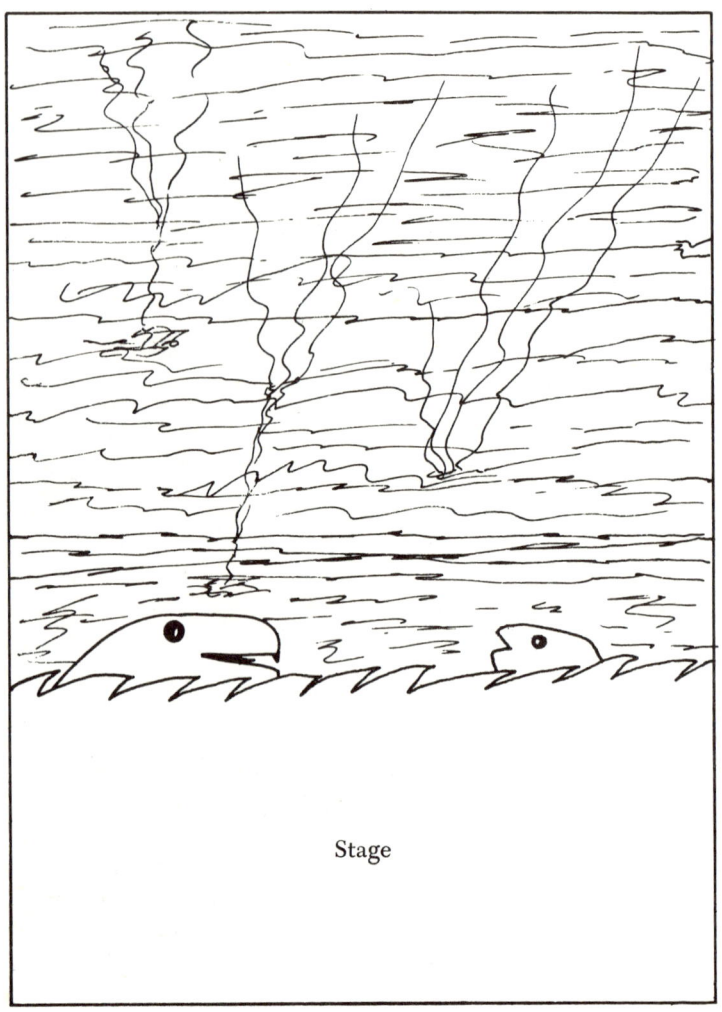

3

Hand Puppets

Although many different kinds of puppets can be bought in the stores, especially clown and animal puppets, there is a limit to the variety, as well as a limit to the amount of money that one wishes to lay out for them. Almost anything can be made into a charming puppet and can be put to work delivering God's good news of salvation.

The puppeteer will naturally become an avid collector of bits of junk. Things other people throw out are the source of life for your puppets: empty cartons; pill boxes; cardboard rolls from paper towels; old tennis balls; Ping Pong balls; carrots; hard bread rolls; apples; tin cans (be sure the sharp edges are covered with adhesive tape); styrofoam balls; blown egg shells; lumps of clay or putty, round, square, oblong, pointed or freeform. If you can stick it over your finger or hand, you have a puppet.

Bits of shiny foil, beads, buttons, bottle tops, and rickrack, become eyebrows, eyes, noses, mouths, teeth, as well as decorations for the puppet's clothes. To make a puppet, all you need is imagination and a houseful of odds and ends.

These puppets have unlimited use in presenting Bible stories, or making announcements, or in teaching verses or songs to the children. For example, the barrel of meal and the cruse of oil could tell how God miraculously kept one family filled during Elijah's time (1 Ki 17:14; see fig. 3a).

These nonhuman types of puppets can be used to make announcements for Christmas or Thanksgiving offerings, or for birthday offerings. For example, many of the smaller children do not understand what happens to the offerings that they bring to Sunday school, or what happens to the money that they put in the birthday bank when they have their birthdays. These could well be explained via the puppet's mouth.

At the end of this chapter you will find a suggested skit for the birthday offering and one for making announcements for the Thanksgiving offering.

The puppets with the widest use are probably the ones that look human. These can be easily made out of prepared commercial "instant" papier-maché. Making the papier-maché puppet heads is perhaps the least difficult of all the tasks associated with puppetry, and certainly one of the more interesting. You do not need to be a sculptor or an artist to make a life-like head.

Instant papier-maché is available at all art stores and many hobby shops. It is excellent material and inexpensive; therefore, it is no longer practical for one to make his own papier-maché. It is possible to make it, of course, and recipes are available in hobby books at all libraries, but the time involved in making it more than outweighs the dollar or so that a pound of prepared papier-maché costs.

After you have prepared your papier-maché, set it aside in a covered bowl so that it will be thoroughly moistened throughout. While you are waiting for this (about one hour), prepare the base for your puppet's head. This could be a three-by-five file card rolled to fit around your finger *loosely* (fig. 3b). Fasten this firmly with tape.

There are two ways to go about starting your puppet's head.
1. You can begin by pressing a large ball of papier-maché over this cardboard tube and begin to shape the head.

Hand Puppets

2. You can make a form around this tube of tissues or paper towels (see fig. 3c), and then work your papier-maché over this.

The first way is slightly easier to model; the second method makes a lighter puppet's head when it is finished, and is somewhat easier to handle. Experiment. Papier-maché is inexpensive. Find out for yourself which method suits you.

Your workbench can be a sheet of waxed paper spread out on your kitchen table. You will need a bowl of warm water to rinse your fingers and tools, an old towel to wipe excess papier-maché from your hands and tools, and some "tools" for sculpturing—a paring knife, a wooden kitchen match or toothpicks, and a teaspoon.

Don't be afraid of the papier-maché. You can rework it if you do not let it sit too long, and after your puppet's head is made and dried and you decide you do not like it, then you have not wasted much time or money, and you have gained valuable experience.

Take a glob and press it around the tube of cardboard or around the tightly packed and tied paper tissues. A good-sized puppet head, that is easy for the performer to handle and easy for the audience to see, should measure about nine inches in circumference. You will want to make it a bit larger if you are making an "adult" head, and you must remember that papier-maché will shrink as it dries.

Heads are not round, most heads are slightly egg shaped, and have a slight bulge at the back (fig. 3d). If you are making a child's face, the features should be below the mid-line of the head (fig. 3e). An adult's features should begin well above mid-line (fig. 3f). A child's ears are small; the older a person gets the larger the ears are usually.

If you are making Caucasian features, the profile runs fairly straight (fig. 3g); that is, the chin and forehead are usually on about the same line. If you are making an African-featured puppet, the profile usually runs something like the drawing of figure 3h.

As your puppet appears before an audience, he will laugh and cry, talk and be silent; so his face must be "in neutral." He must be neither too happy looking or too sad. Make the mouth slightly opened.

Use your paring knife, match, and spoon to press the papier-maché into place and form the features. Be sure to add ears, and remember that ears are usually on the level with mid-eye. Observe people; see how their ears are placed, where their eyebrows are; and notice the shape of their mouths.

Don't worry about your puppet's face and head being rough. When the papier-maché dries it can be smoothed with fine sandpaper if you wish, or it can be left rough. Leaving it fairly rough gives a more lifelike texture to the puppets who are supposed to be human looking.

Forming the eyes should give you no problem. Make eye sockets in the wet papier-maché, and then roll small egg-shaped bits of papier-maché and press them into the sockets.

As you form the neck of your puppet leave a small ridge around the bottom (fig. 3i). This will give you a firm place on which you can glue the puppet's body.

When you have finished your puppet's head, set it aside to dry. Be careful not to lay it on its side, but stick the puppet over the narrow neck of a bottle or something else with a firm base, so that the papier-maché will not be pressed out of shape (fig. 3j).

How to Paint the Head

When your puppet is completely dry, (about 48-72 hours) it can be painted with either oil paints or poster (tempera) paints. Poster paints are cheaper and easier to use and entirely

Hand Puppets

satisfactory. Skin tones will give you some difficulty, and even the "flesh-colored" prepared paints will probably have to be doctored by adding white, pink, or perhaps a trace of yellow. Once again, experiment.

If you don't like your finished product, it is easy to repaint. When using poster paints, you must use two coats anyway. Paint the skin first—the entire head and eyeballs—all the same color. Let it dry—two hours should be long enough—then repaint the complete head. After the second coat, you are ready to put in the features. If you have made your puppet's mouth slightly open, then paint the inside red. When it is dry, you can add a few light touches of white to simulate teeth. Paint the lips. Look at the color of people's lips; they are not all bright red. If your characters are to play lifelike roles you will want them to be as nearly lifelike as possible.

Painting the eyes should not cause any trouble. The eyes will probably be slightly larger in proportion to the rest of the body. This will make them easier for the audience to see. After the complete eyeball is painted white, add the lid. It is rare that one sees the complete iris of a person's eye, and an older person is apt to have more of his iris covered than a child (figs. 3k and 3l). Paint the iris, the colored part of the eye, in the center of the eyeball. You do not want your puppet to be continually looking out of the corner of his eye. To make the eye seem more natural and larger, put a small red dot right at the corner of the eye towards the nose (figs. 3k and 3l). Do not try to paint a white highlight onto the eye. After the puppet is finished, you can cover the eye with clear nail polish and this will give your puppet's eye a lifelike glint.

The puppet's hair can either be painted or glued on. Black velvet will make an African man's hair; black yarn will make a woman's. You might want to scalp an old doll and use its hair for your puppet.

Making the Body

Making the body seems as though it should be the simplest part of puppetry. Actually, it is probably the most difficult, for the body must be loose enough for the performer's hand to fit in comfortably, and tight enough to keep the performer's fingers and thumbs from slipping out of the "arms." The beginning puppeteer will be worried because his puppet's body is misshapen; one shoulder will be lower than the other (fig. 3*m*). This is characteristic of the hand puppet and cannot be helped. This is caused by the shape of the performer's hand. It will be well not to try to compensate for this in making the body of your puppet. Make both shoulders of equal height. This is the way puppets are and there is nothing that can be done about it. You and the children to whom you present your story will learn to love these misshapen little characters.

The cloth for the body should be of material that is comfortable on your hand. Avoid stiff taffetalike or heavily starched material. Soft knits, old tee shirts, or babies' underwear makes excellent body material. You can dye the material to suit the color of your character. A white person is not white; a black person is not black.

The puppet body must be slightly larger than the breadth of the performer's hand. The puppet's arms are about half as long as the performer's thumb. Make the neck of the body large enough to fit over the ridge on the puppet's head. Glue and tie this tightly so that your puppet does not lose his head in the middle of the play. (See fig. 3*n*).

How to Dress Your Puppet

Study the costumes of people of other lands if you are going to use your puppet for missionary plays. The costumes do not need to be elaborate, merely the suggestion of a style is sufficient. A long sari for an Indian woman can be an oblong piece

Hand Puppets

of silk cloth, an African man's robe can be an oblong piece of cloth with a hole in the middle for the neck (fig. 3*o*).

Puppets, by the way, are always dressed from the bottom. Do not try to make necklines large enough to slip over your puppet's head.

The clothes should be loose fitting and slightly larger than the puppet's body so that they do not restrict the free movement of the performer's hands. Once again, avoid stiff or starchy material. Avoid large patterns; they should be in scale with the puppet's size.

Because your puppet does not have legs, your man puppet cannot wear trousers, so only the suggestion of trousers can be made. Remember that the bottom of the puppet's body is always below the eye level of the audience anyway. (See figure 3*p*).

If your children's group uses a birthday-cake bank for birthday offerings, the following skit could be used to show the purpose of it.

BIRTHDAY CAKE

CHARACTERS: Birthday Cake (see fig. 3*q*)
            Girl (paper bag)
            Boy (paper bag)

GIRL: Yesterday was my birthday. I'm going to put six pennies in the birthday cake today.

BOY: Hey, that's funny! Yesterday was my birthday, too. I've got seven pennies Mother gave me to put in the cake. But— but—I don't know. Seven pennies is a lot of money. But—

CAKE: But what?

BOY: Oh! I didn't see you come in. Hey, I never heard of a talking birthday cake!

CAKE: Lots of things you never heard of. So suppose you ask me anything you want to know, and I'll tell you.

GIRL: Are you THAT smart?

Boy: You just want to eat all our pennies, that's all.

Cake: Oh, so that's what's bothering you. Well, let me tell you what happens to those birthday pennies you put in me. Say, did you get any presents yesterday?

Girl: I got a new doll and skates!

Boy: I had a party, and I got lots of presents—games, balls, a new sweater. But what are you asking for? YOU were supposed to tell ME what you do with all those pennies.

Girl: My Sunday school teacher said they were for Jesus.

Boy: Yeah, but how does HE get them?

Cake: Let me tell you. You know that missionary who was here a few weeks ago?

Boy: Yes.

Cake: Well, when I get full of pennies, then the Sunday school teacher takes them all and sends them out to the missionary.

Girl: But she said they were for Jesus!

Cake: That's who they are for. You see, there are lots of little boys and girls in (name of any country) who have never heard about Jesus. So the missionary uses your pennies to buy books and Sunday school papers to give to these boys and girls that will tell them about Jesus.

Boy: So when they read about Jesus in these papers, then—then—they learn to love Him. Is that it?

Girl: And when they learn about Jesus and love Him—Hey! that's really giving to Jesus, isn't it?

Boy: I wish I was a hundred years old, then I could put in a whole dollar!

Cake: You could slip in an extra dime, if you wanted to.

Boy: Hey! How did you know I had a dime?

Cake: I'm smart.

Boy: I'll do it. I want some other boy to know about Jesus.

Cake: Happy birthday!

Boy: You know, it really is a happy birthday when you let others know about Jesus.

Hand Puppets

Fig. 3a. Barrel and cruse-of-oil puppets

Poke hole in bottom, insert handkerchief-covered finger.

Barrel made out of paper cup

Cruse of oil made from water pitcher

Insert cloth-covered fist into inverted water pitcher.

Figs. 3*b*-3*d*. Head of papier-maché puppet

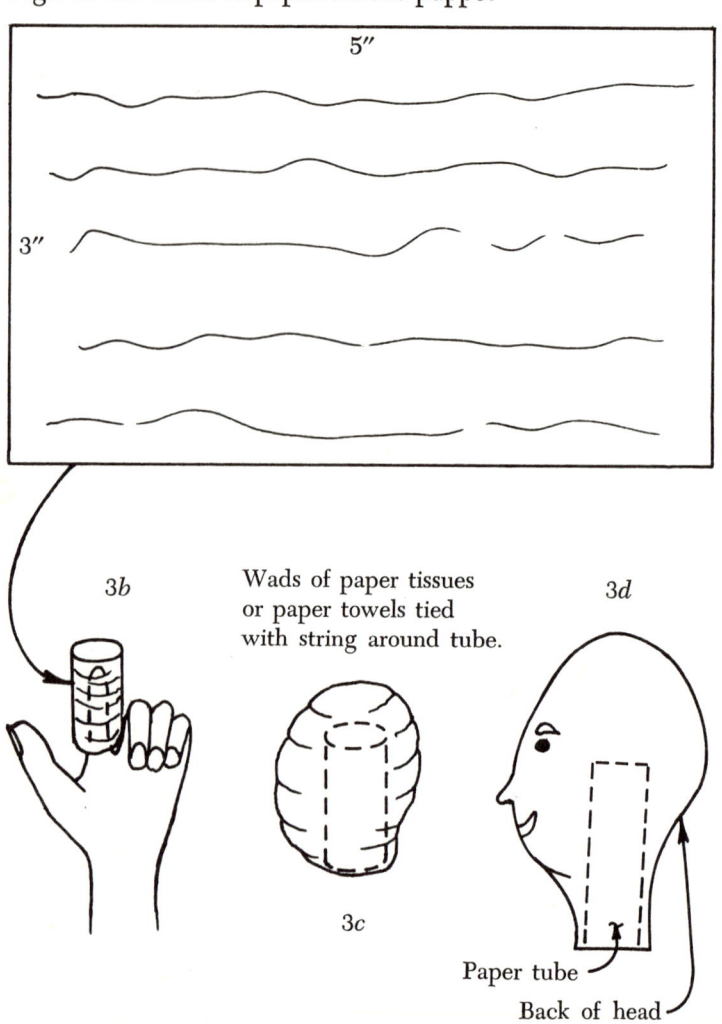

5″

3″

3b

Wads of paper tissues or paper towels tied with string around tube.

3c

3d

Paper tube
Back of head

Hand Puppets 41

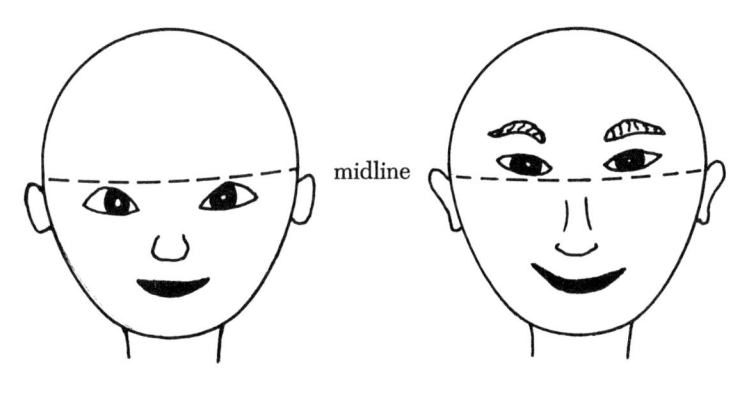

midline

Fig. 3*e*. Child

Fig. 3*f*. Adult

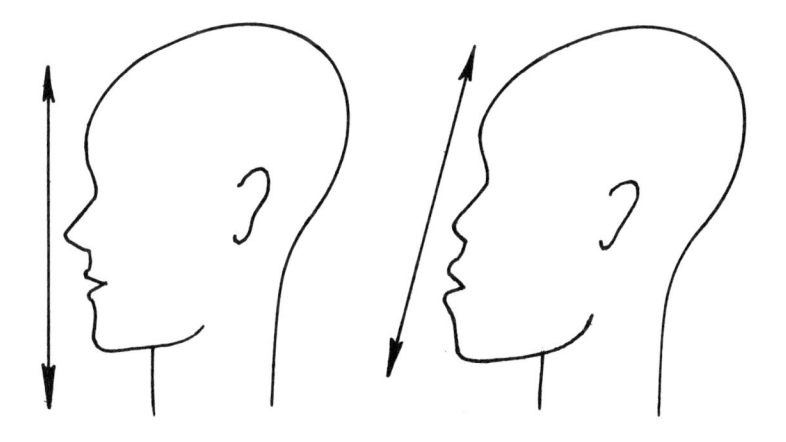

Fig. 3*g*. Caucasian

Fig. 3*h*. African

42 *You Can Be a Puppeteer!*

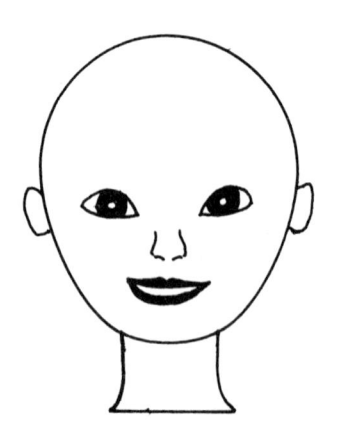

Fig. 3i. Ridge at neck edge

Fig. 3j. Letting the head dry

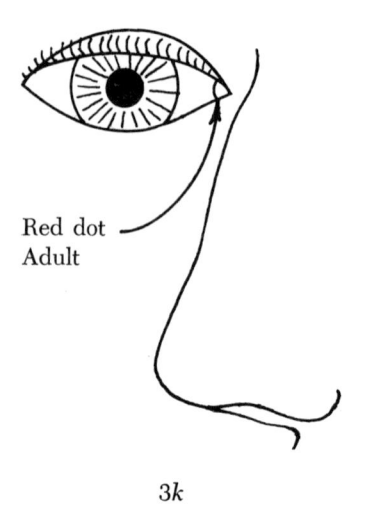

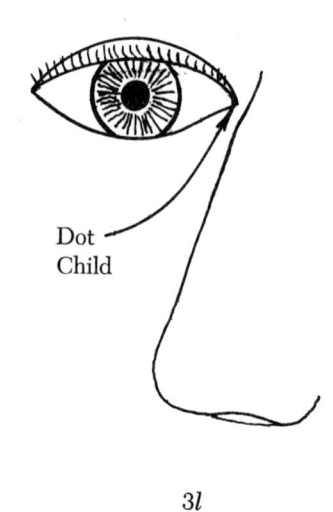

Red dot
Adult

Dot
Child

3k

3l

Figs. 3k-3l. Eyes

Hand Puppets 43

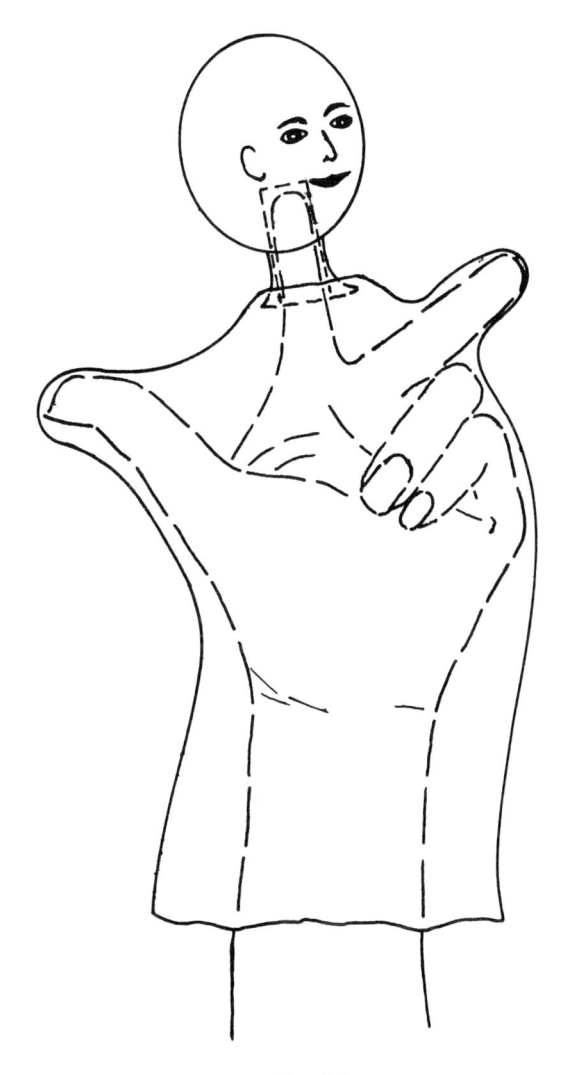

Fig. 3*m*. Shoulders

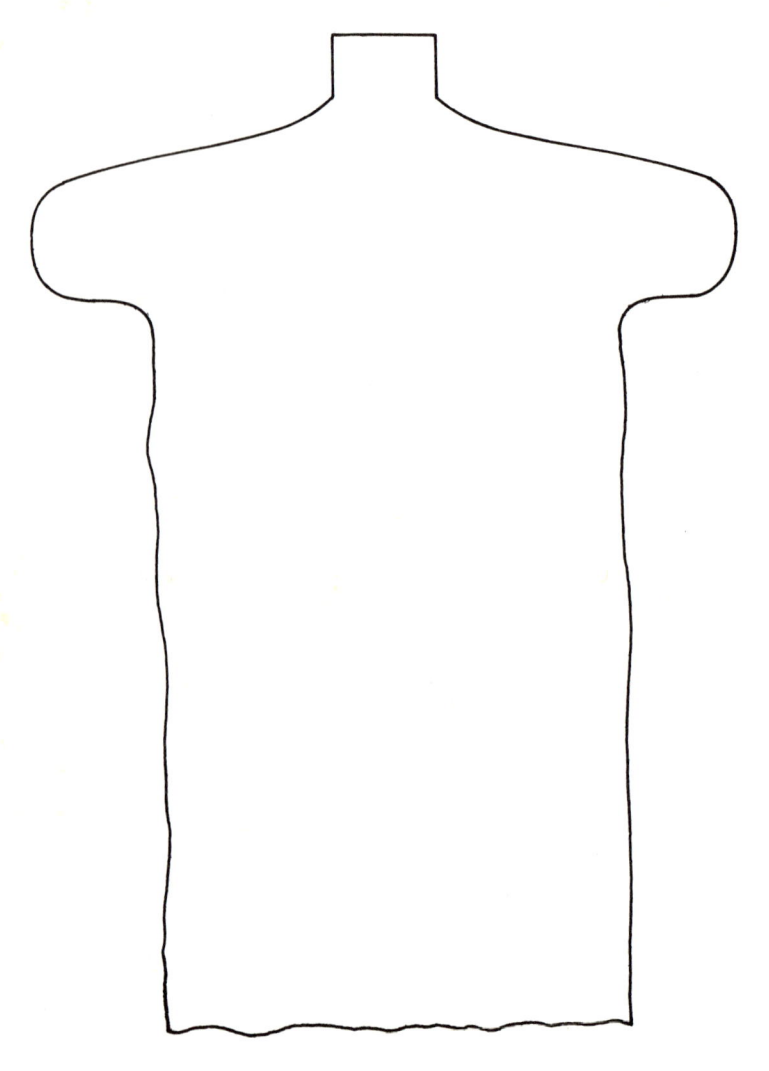

Fig. 3n. Suggested pattern for puppet body

Hand Puppets

Fig. 3o. Simple robe

Fig. 3p. Man puppet

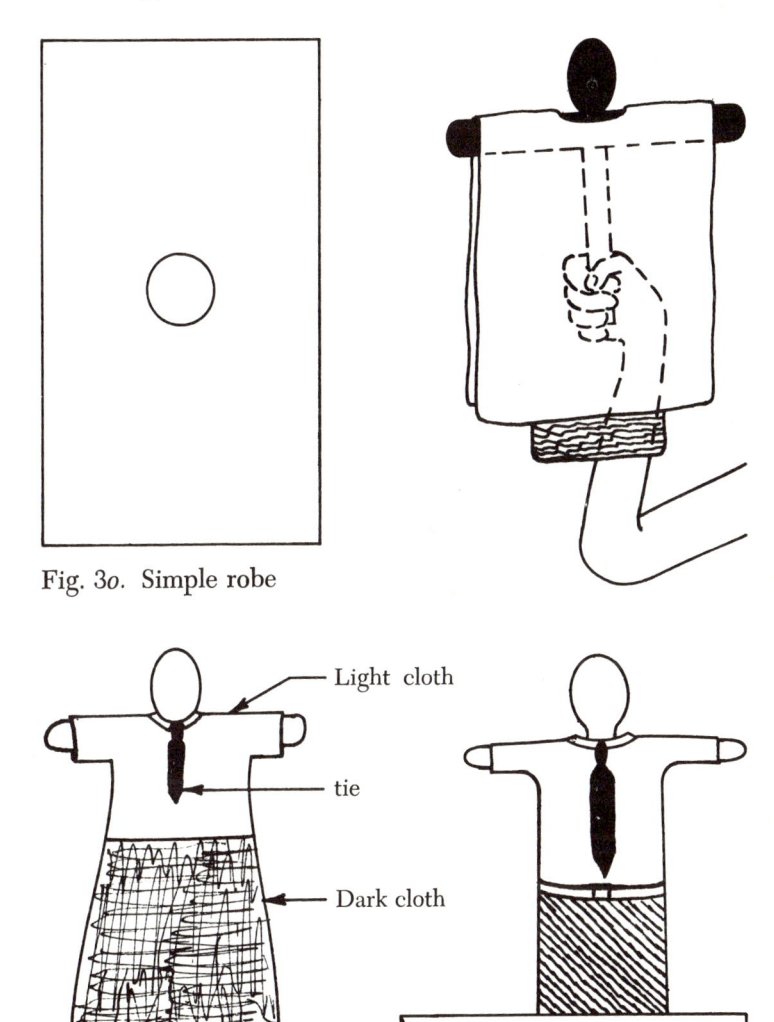

- Light cloth
- tie
- Dark cloth

Stage

You Can Be a Puppeteer!

Happy Birthday

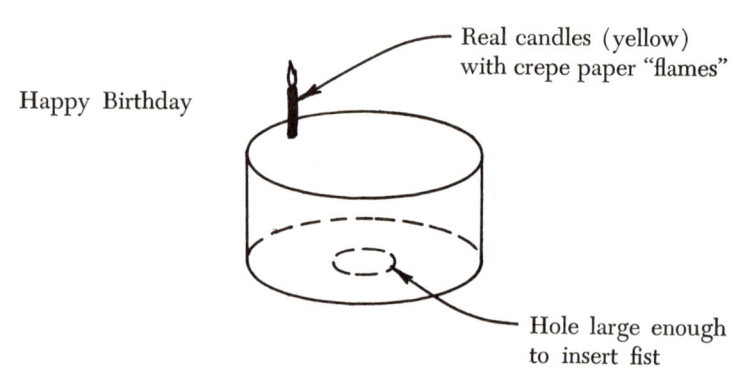

Real candles (yellow) with crepe paper "flames"

Hole large enough to insert fist

Use a bath powder-type box with lid glued on. Cover with crepe paper or paint to resemble a birthday cake.

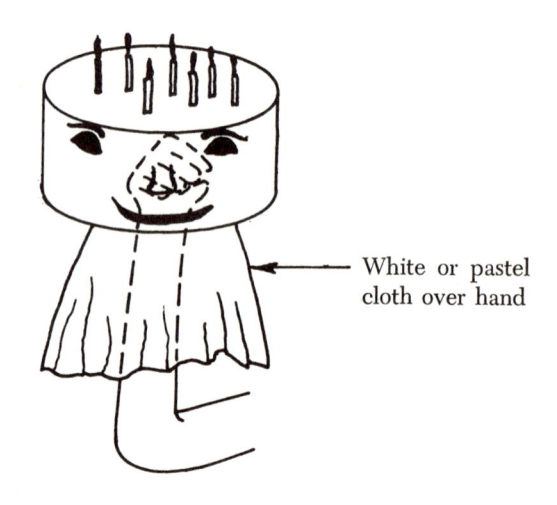

White or pastel cloth over hand

Fig. 3q. Birthday cake puppet

4

How to Make Your Puppet Come Alive

Action is the secret of puppetry. And yet, the action must have meaning. Senseless bobbing around of the puppet will only confuse the audience. A puppet's message is given to the audience by two things: your voice and the action that your hands give. Therefore, you must make your puppet not only talk as he is supposed to, but move as he is supposed to. A braggart swaggers; a thief slinks; an old man wobbles; a happy child skips; a stubborn child drags his feet and moves slowly; a frightened child runs or hides; a blind person gropes, sliding his feet and extending his hands. Your puppets must *do* something. They may move across the stage; they may hit each other (puppets are notorious fighters!); they may rub their heads or hide their faces; but they must do something. When one puppet "speaks" he must move either his head or his hands, or sometimes both, and the other puppet must be still, so as not to detract from the speaker.

Practically any story can be adapted to a puppet play if it has enough action. Short skits do not need violent action, longer plays do.

Actions That Are Suitable for Hand Puppets

1. bending over or bowing
2. dodging blows

3. hitting or beating someone or something
4. hiding something
5. chopping down trees, or firewood, etc.
6. hoeing ground or sweeping
7. pointing to something
8. rubbing head or stomach as though hungry or in pain
9. eating, moving hand to mouth and back to dish
10. touching another person or object
11. moving something from one place to another
12. pushing or pulling something
13. walking, running, crawling, hopping

The most important movement for your puppet is walking. This requires three distinct movements: the bending of your wrist in a right-left direction, a slight upward-downward movement, and a forward movement of the whole arm at the same time. (See Introduction, figs. *b* and *c*.)

To make your puppet "bow," bend the wrist forward slightly. Your fingers, in the puppet's arms, will add to the illusion, if you fold the thumb in front of the puppet's body and make a graceful sweep with the other "arm" by moving your middle finger (fig. 4*a*).

To make him clap his hands, merely bring the thumb and middle finger together rapidly and repeatedly. The head must be held firmly so that it will not wobble unnecessarily.

Kicking can be simulated by a quick movement of the palm of the hand at the same time twisting the hand slightly either to the left or right, depending on which "foot" is supposed to be kicking. Remember, your hand puppets do not have legs, so the illusion of legs must be carried out by the performer's quick and sure movements.

Your puppet does have hands, but they are fingerless stumps. This can be compensated for. He can pick up things with one hand if you have little hooks embedded in the object he is to

How to Make Your Puppet Come Alive 49

pick up (fig. 4b). A bent straight pin glued or fastened into the object will allow it to cling to his hand. It can be removed either by another puppet using two hands, or by a quick twist of your finger when the puppet wants to set it down.

Your ill-tempered puppet can slap or hit another puppet by swinging either your thumb or middle finger. He may pick up a stick with both hands and beat something or someone. Or he can be a loving, gentle puppet, and pat someone or something gently on the head.

It is essential that you be comfortable when presenting your puppet show. You have to have freedom to move, so you must wear comfortable, loose-fitting clothes. A blouse or shirt or coat that does not allow quick and easy movement is not the proper dress for a puppeteer.

Your puppet is clothed; he can move; now you must learn to make him talk. A short, simple skit can be done by one person, if there are no more than two puppets to manage. You must remember to raise your voice to a higher pitch for a child's part, and lower it for an adult. Try to change the tone and pitch of your voice. This will take practice. When you have achieved the proper "voice" for each character, you make them "talk" by moving the puppet who is speaking. You will be hidden when you present your puppet play, so you do not need to worry about ventriloquism. Your "speaking" puppet must move his head slightly, and the other puppets *must be still.*

Almost everyone has access these days to a tape recorder, so it is possible for you to record your play before you present it. This will free you to concentrate on the movements of your puppets during the performance. It will also give you time to perfect your two-voice presentation.

If you record your play, then you will need an assistant to start the recorder for you when you are ready to perform. It is advisable to have the recorder where it is not easily seen, so that it will not distract the children from the performance.

However, the recorder should be in a place where it is easily heard. You don't want to hide it in back of heavy curtains that will muffle the sound.

The Stage

A puppet that walks and talks must have a place to perform. This is your stage. This stage can be as simple as a table, or it can be an ornate, complicated stage with curtains that open and shut and lights that dim. The size and type of stage will depend on where you intend to put on your puppet shows and how often. At the end of this chapter several suggestions for easily constructed puppet stages are illustrated.

Most professional puppeteers seem to prefer to work their puppets by holding them over their heads (fig. 4c). This gives greater freedom to the puppets, if you can do it. However, it is very tiring, and unless you have had long years of practice holding your hands over your head and working with the puppets, you will find it almost impossible to do.

I work seated on a straight chair. I have a light, semitransparent curtain between me and the audience. I dress in dark clothes and occasionally wear a dark veil over my face so that the children cannot see any reflection of my glasses or the white of my face. I have a dark curtain covering my working area. (See fig. 4d.) Such an elaborate setup is not necessary for an occasional puppet presentation.

How to Make Your Puppet Come Alive 51

Fig. 4*a*. Your puppet bows

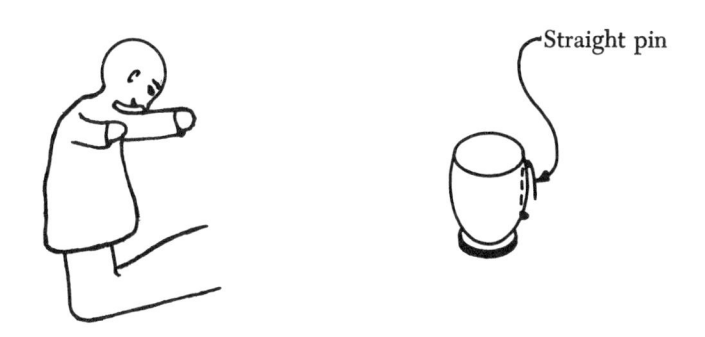

Straight pin

Fig. 4*b*. Object to be picked up

Fig. 4*c*. Rear view

52   *You Can Be a Puppeteer!*

Fig. 4d. Author's stage, working area

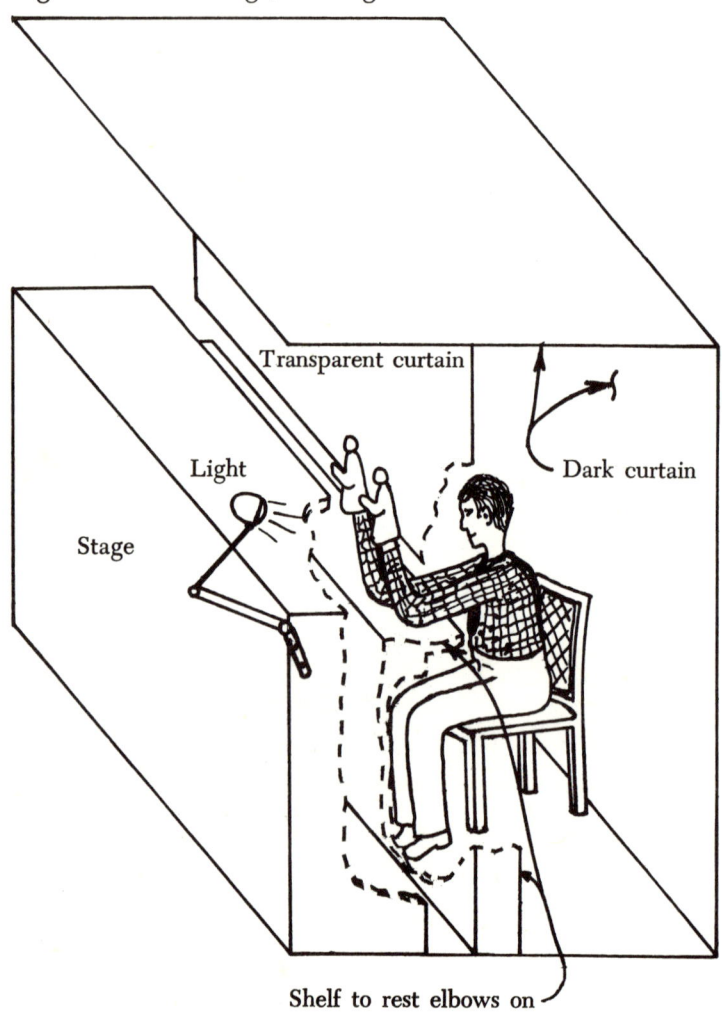

How to Make Your Puppet Come Alive

Figs. 4e-4h. Suggestions for puppet stages

4e Doorway

Curtain

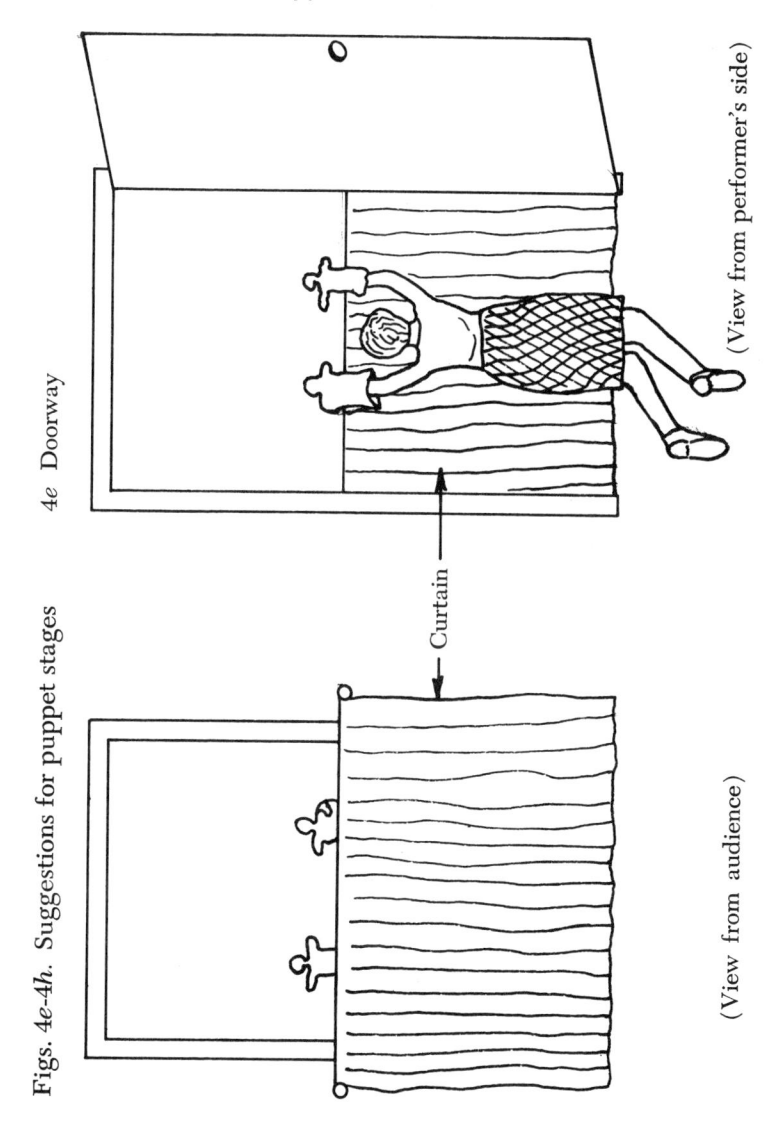

(View from performer's side)

(View from audience)

54   *You Can Be a Puppeteer!*

4*f* Table or desk

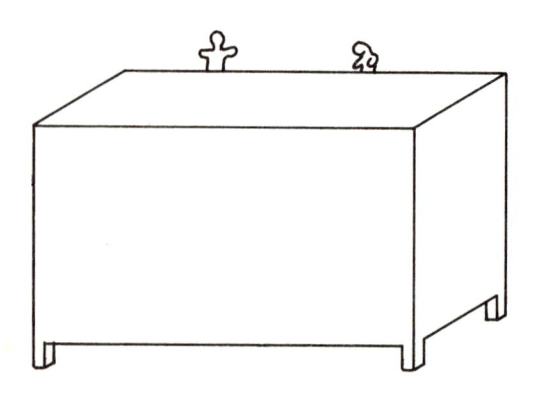

(View from audience)

(View from performer's side)

How to Make Your Puppet Come Alive 55

4g Table or desk

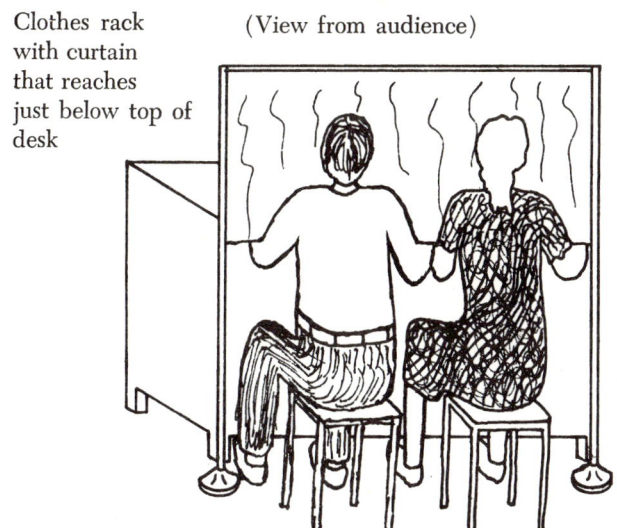

Clothes rack
with curtain
that reaches
just below top of
desk

(View from audience)

56 *You Can Be a Puppeteer!*

4h Desk

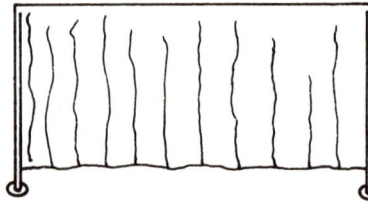

Puppets

Curtain on frame set on desk

Long box placed on desk to act as stage

Part II

PLAYS

5

The Play

Children have been conditioned to expect funny things to happen in puppet shows, such as magic, and talking animals, and slapstick comedy. This type of play has its place, but it is difficult to present in a serious missionary or Bible story. Humor has a definite role in teaching, even in teaching the Bible, but one must be careful not to make light of sacred things.

Your serious puppet play should be kept short, should have as much action as possible, and should present the truth that you want to get across to the children as clearly and concisely as possible in the speech of the actors and with no long moralizing sermon at the end. The message must be incorporated into the body of the play.

You will want to develop your own plays. You will find suggestions for puppet plays in almost any missionary's letter if you study it. Perhaps they didn't outline it as a play, but it will have the germ thought that you need to present some truth to the children.

Is your missionary writing to thank you for the gift of money you sent him? Did he spend it for gas for his car? Develop a play showing how he used the car to take the gospel to someone who had never heard. Did she spend it for medicine? Tell, in your play, how someone heard the story of Jesus when they came to the hospital.

When planning your puppet show you must keep the following in mind:

1. The point you want to get across. Develop only one point for each play. If you want to tell children how to witness to their school friends, keep it to that. Do not bring in tithing, or prayer—as important as those things are.
2. The age of your audience.
3. How many characters will be needed to perform the play. It is better not to have more than four puppets, using two puppeteers.

Four things make a good puppet play:

1. Suspense. Your audience must always wonder, What's coming next?
2. A problem to solve. How will the hero work out this problem?
3. Your characters. If it is a lifelike story, they must be plausible and the conversation natural and believable.
4. Plenty of action.

Certain Bible stories lend themselves well to puppet plays.

1. The Good Samaritan has plenty of action with the thieves beating the traveler, the Good Samaritan putting him on his donkey after giving him treatment, taking him to the inn, etc. And, of course, show all the others walking by and not helping the poor man.
2. The Lost Coin shows the woman sweeping her house, bending over to look for the coin, calling the neighbors who rejoice when she's found it.
3. David and Goliath needs no explanation.
4. Samson pulls down the house and kills the Philistines.
5. Balaam's ass talks and he smites her.
6. Jonah and the whale (see chapter 3).

The Play

7. Joseph is put in the well, and then drawn out and sold by his brothers.

You will find that your little puppets will not only bring you hours of enjoyment as you learn to manipulate them, but they will help make the precious truths of His Word and His work more real to the little ones in your Sunday school and Bible classes.

6

Broken Windshield

(A Missionary Story from India)

PUPPET PLAY FOR ONE PERFORMER

CHARACTERS: MUNDU: garden boy
NOKER: cook
MISSIONARY

PROPS: two-story house   tree
Jeep or other toy car   bundle of wood
ax   garden
waterpot   slingshot

DIRECTIONS FOR MAKING HOUSE

Take a flat piece of cardboard (poster board or the top of a suit box can be used), and draw the outline of a two-story house with windows and doors. (See Figs. 6a-6c.) The size of the house depends on the dimensions of your stage. The house does not have to be perfectly made, nor in proportion to the puppet figures. Props in puppet shows merely suggest the background to the audience.

COSTUMING

MUNDU is dressed in light-colored clothes with a brightly-colored blanket over his shoulder. NOKER, the cook, has a cook's

Broken Windshield 63

hat (this can be the toe section of a child's white sock) and a white apron.

(SCENE ONE: *Curtain opens to find* Mundu *playing with slingshot. He has to hold slingshot with both hands.*)

Noker (*steps out of the house and yells*): Put that slingshot away and bring me some water.

Mundu: I'm busy. I'm working in the garden, Noker.

Noker: You are playing with that slingshot. You are a lazy boy! I do not see why the missionary gave you that slingshot. He even gave you that blanket. He should have given me a blanket.

Mundu: He gave you one last month, Noker.

Noker: Well, he shouldn't have given you one. Now bring me some water from the well. Mundu! Bring me water!

Mundu: I have my own work to do.

Noker: Stop playing with that slingshot. The missionary told you not to play with it near the house.

Mundu: I'm not shooting it. I'm just looking at it.

Noker: Mundu, you'd better get some water for me or—or—

Mundu: Or what, Mr. Noker? Remember what the missionary said. He said everyone should do his own work.

Noker: I don't see you working! Besides, you couldn't hit anything with that slingshot. You're too dumb! (*Enters house.*)

Mundu: Dumb! I'm not dumb! Old Noker is the dumb one! I'll bet I can hit anything I want to with this slingshot! I'll bet I can hit that tree. Noker couldn't hit anything. HE'S too dumb. I can hit that tree. (*Raises hands and moves them around as though he is twirling a stone in the slingshot.*) There's no one around to see me. (*Stops and looks.*) No one in the house. Old Noker's back in the kitchen. There's no one over there. (*Nods head to right.*) No one over there. (*Looks to left.*) No one will ever know. (*Swings arms around again.*) No one will know. (*Moves arm back and holds it as though he has thrown stone; sound of glass breaking; long pause.*) Oho! I—I broke the missionary's car window. Oho! Oho! (*Drops slingshot; hides head in arms; rocks back and forth as though in pain.*) Oh, I shall die! Oh, what will happen to me? The missionary will be angry. Oh-oh, his nice new car! (*Moves forward slowly toward the car, hands on head, moaning as he moves.*) Oh, what shall I do? (*Looks around anxiously.*) The missionary will be angry. (*Looks at tree.*) Hmm, one of those branches is dying. Hmm, I wonder. If the missionary thought the branch fell on the car, then he would never know I broke the window. (*Reaches up and yanks the branch loose and lays it over the top of the car; steps back and admires his work.*) Hmm, no one will ever know. (*Turns to "garden" and stoops down to begin work.*)

NOKER (*stepping out of house*): Mundu! Mundu, bring me some water and then chop some wood for me!

MUNDU: Chop your own wood. I'm busy.

NOKER: If you don't chop wood for me and get water, I will tell the missionary.

MUNDU: Tell him? Tell him what?

NOKER: I will tell him that you broke his windshield.

MUNDU: You what! I—how did you know—no one saw. I mean —I didn't—the wind did.

NOKER: You broke his windshield with your slingshot. Then you put the branch on it, you did!

(MUNDU *shakes his head as though to deny it.*)

NOKER: Go on, get water for me, or— Hurry!

MUNDU (*gets up, moves towards waterpots*): But how did you know? I looked all around.

NOKER (*laughing*): I was upstairs. I looked out the window and saw you. Bring the water!

(MUNDU *picks up the water jar and carries it to* NOKER *who re-*

Broken Windshield 65

ceives it from his hands. NOKER *enters house and returns without the jar.*)

NOKER: Now bring me some wood. Hurry!

MUNDU: I—I've got my own work to do.

NOKER: Hurry. I'll tell the missionary and he'll put you in jail. Or maybe you can pay for that windshield?

MUNDU: Oh, Noker, never in a thousand years could I pay for that windshield. I am too poor. Where would I get money to do this?

NOKER: Get some wood for me. Hurry.

(MUNDU *runs and picks up the ax and begins to "chop" wood. Curtain closes.*)

(SCENE TWO: *Curtain opens to find* MUNDU *working in the garden.* NOKER *enters.*)

NOKER: Mundu, I need some more water. Hurry!

MUNDU: Oh, Noker, have mercy. For five days now I have had no rest. The missionary wants his garden weeded. You want wood and water, and your pots and pans washed. Have mercy!

NOKER: I am having mercy. Have I told the missionary about the terrible thing you did?

MUNDU: No, but I cannot do your work, I am so tired.

NOKER: You will do what I say, or I will tell the missionary. If I tell him, then he will put you in jail, because you cannot pay for your sin.

MUNDU: Yesterday in church, yesterday the missionary said God would forgive us if we confessed our sins.

NOKER: But the missionary, he is a man. God will forgive, but not the missionary. Bring me some wood. Hurry.

MUNDU: Oh, Noker, I am so tired.

NOKER: Bring wood. Bring water, hurry. I will tell the missionary, and he will put you in jail. (*Enters house.*)

MUNDU (*sits down, hands on head*): Oh, I am so sad. I am so sad. If I tell the missionary he will put me in jail. If I don't tell him, then Noker will kill me with work. I am so sad. Oh-oh, oh-oh, I am so sad.

MISSIONARY (*enters from inside the house*): Mundu, you look unhappy. What is bothering you?

MUNDU: Oh, missionary, I am so sad.

MISSIONARY (*moves toward* MUNDU *and pats him on the head*): Lately you have not been happy. I have missed your happy singing. And your face looks so sad and unhappy.

MUNDU: Missionary, please don't put me in jail. Please, I have no money to pay you, and I am so sad. Please don't put me in jail.

MISSIONARY: Tell me what you have done. Why should I put you in jail?

MUNDU: Oh, Missionary, I am so sorry. I have done something very wrong. (*Bows before* MISSIONARY *and sobs. This can be done by making him shake.*)

MISSIONARY: Mundu, don't cry.

MUNDU: Missionary, I broke your car window, and I put the branch on it to make it look like the wind did it. Now—now you know, and you will put me in jail. I can't pay for it. I could never pay for it.

MISSIONARY: Oh, Mundu, I know you broke it. But, the windshield is already paid for. I have ordered a new one from the garage.

MUNDU (*sitting up in alarm*): You knew I broke it? But—but—Noker said if you knew you would put me in jail. How did you know?

MISSIONARY: I did not know that Noker knew you had broken it. I was upstairs, and I saw you from the window. I called a warning to you, but you did not hear me. And I saw you break it. I have been waiting to hear you say that you were sorry. Now that you have said it, that is all that counts.

MUNDU: You mean—you mean, I am forgiven?

MISSIONARY: You know, it is what the Bible says we should do

Broken Windshield

when we sin against God. We should ask Jesus to forgive us. When we do this, Jesus forgives our sins. I just wanted to hear you say that you were sorry.

MUNDU: I sinned and you forgave me. Is that what Jesus will do, too?

MISSIONARY: If you tell Him that you are sorry for your sins.

MUNDU: Oh, Missionary, I want to tell Jesus I am sorry that I have not believed Him. (*Folds hands and bows head.*) Dear Jesus, I am sorry. Thank You for forgiving me. I have heard about You, but I didn't believe You would forgive me. Now I believe. I'm sorry for my sins. Forgive me. Amen. Now, Missionary, I am happy.

MISSIONARY: Good, it will be nice to hear your happy singing again. I have work to do, so I will go inside now. (*Leaves.*)

(MUNDU *begins singing and walks over to garden and begins to work in the garden. Change puppets on hand and bring* NOKER *out.*)

NOKER: Mundu! Bring me some wood!

MUNDU: No, Noker, get your own wood. I have to work in the garden.

NOKER: I shall tell the missionary, and he will put you in jail.

MUNDU: No, Noker, he will not put me in jail. You see, he has forgiven me.

NOKER: Forgiven you?

MUNDU: Yes, I told him I was sorry, and he forgave me. He's already bought a new windshield. You know, Noker, that's just what we've been hearing in church. Remember, the missionary said God had already paid for our sins? Well, today I asked Jesus to forgive me and I believe Him. And I asked the missionary to forgive me, so I'm twice forgiven! You know, Noker, you ought to ask Jesus to forgive you, too.

(*Curtain closes.*)

68   *You Can Be a Puppeteer!*

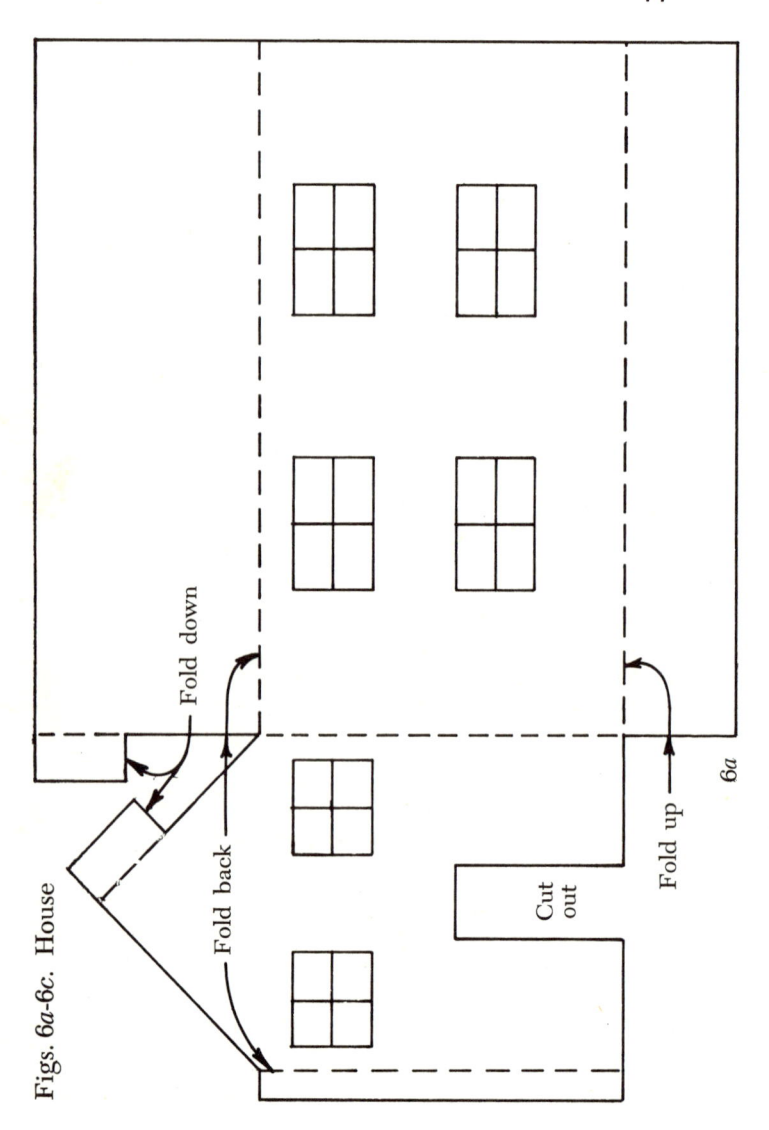

Figs. 6a-6c. House

Fold down

Fold back

Fold up

Cut out

6a

Broken Windshield 69

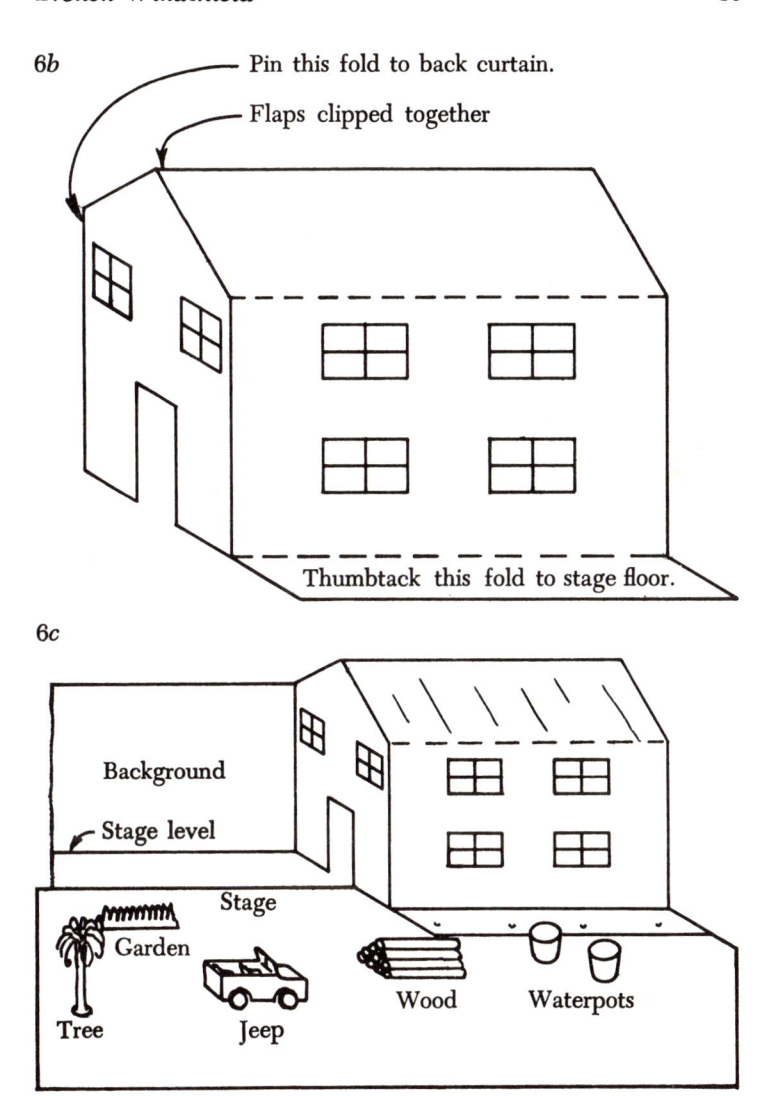

6b

— Pin this fold to back curtain.

— Flaps clipped together

Thumbtack this fold to stage floor.

6c

Background

Stage level

Stage

Tree Garden Jeep Wood Waterpots

70   *You Can Be a Puppeteer!*

Fig. 6*d*. Tree of wires tied together

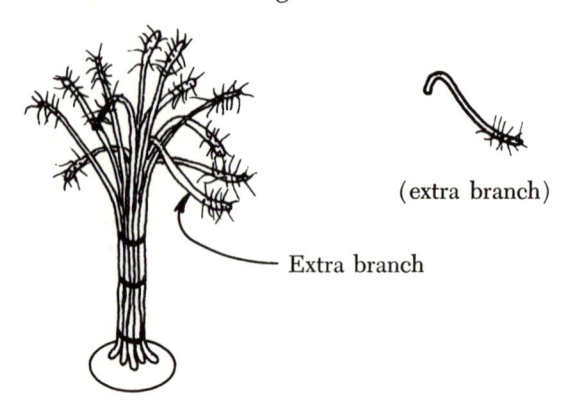

(extra branch)

Extra branch

Fig. 6*e*. Garden

Green crepe paper

Papier-mâché or clay or plasticine

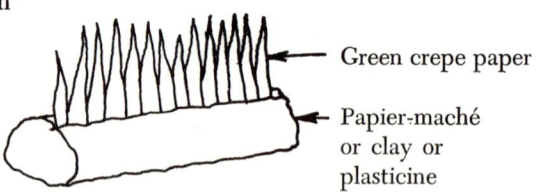

Fig. 6*f*. Slingshot

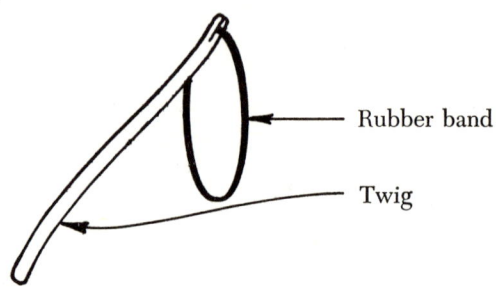

Rubber band

Twig

7

Baby Moses

Puppet Play for Two Performers

Characters

Mother
Pharaoh's daughter } first performer

Miriam
Maid } second performer

Props

Baby: This is a roll of light pink cloth inside a white "blanket." (Size is in proportion to other puppets.)

Two baskets: Same size, same pattern, one of light-colored paper, one of brown or black paper. (See fig. 7a.)

Palm tree: (See fig. 6d.)

Reeds: These are fringed pieces of green crepe paper of various heights inserted into a base of soft modeling clay or plasticine (fig. 7b).

Window: This is made of construction paper and pinned to back curtain (fig. 7d), which should be light blue or gray.

Sound Effect of Crying Baby

This may be on tape, or from a sound effect record. (Many

public libraries have records of sound effects.) If not recorded, then one of the puppeteers may make the crying sounds.

Costuming

MOTHER and MIRIAM should be in dark brown or navy clothes with veils over heads. (Do not cover faces; fig. 7e.) MOTHER should have different colored veil than MIRIAM. MAID'S dress should be brighter color. PHARAOH'S DAUGHTER should have brilliantly colored dress (nylon or rayon jersey makes an excellent dress) and a gaudy headpiece. Make a "cone" of gold paper, cut it in half, and fasten it over a brilliantly colored veil or headscarf. (Fig. 7f.)

(SCENE ONE: *Curtain opens with* MOTHER *and baby in her arms. They are inside house. Baby begins to cry.*)

MOTHER: Oh, my poor baby, what shall I do with you? Hush your crying. (*Rocks back and forth and hums to the baby.*) Hush your crying. Ssh, someone will hear you. (*Baby's cries fade gradually.*) Lovely baby, gift of the great Creator, what shall I do with you? What will happen to you? (MOTHER *begins to sob. Make sobbing sound, and have* MOTHER's *shoulders shake.*) Oh, my poor baby.

MIRIAM (*enters*): Mother, have you heard the latest news? Pharaoh's soldiers have just killed the infant son of Esther. (*Begins to sob.*) Oh, Mother, what, what shall we do? Yesterday three more baby boys were found and killed. (*Moves toward* MOTHER *and baby, touches blanket.*) Oh, my poor baby brother, what shall happen to you? Oh, my sweet baby brother. Let me hold him, Mother. (*Takes baby from* MOTHER.)

MOTHER: Shh! I think he has fallen asleep. Oh, my heart is heavy. Last night I cried all night long and prayed that Jehovah would hear my pleas. I— (*Pauses, looks around fearfully.*) Shh! Did you hear a noise?

Baby Moses

MIRIAM: Oh, Mother! Perhaps it's the soldiers. (*Goes to window and looks out.*) No, Mother, there is no one. (*Returns to* MOTHER'S *side.*)

MOTHER: Every little noise I hear makes my heart afraid. Are you SURE no one's there?

MIRIAM: I saw no one. Oh, Mother, what is going to happen to us? Life is so hard. What are we going to do?

MOTHER: I don't know. Our life is bitter. Pharaoh's men are sure to find our precious baby boy. Your father told me that the soldiers are searching every house. Every baby boy is being thrown into the river. Only the girl babies are allowed to live.

MIRIAM: Old Pharaoh is so mean! I hate him!

MOTHER: Pharaoh has increased the work for all the Hebrew slaves. Imagine! We, the chosen people of the great Jehovah are slaves! And now our sons are killed. Oh, God has dealt harshly with us. God has forgotten His people Israel.

MIRIAM: Mother, tell me again how it all started, about Joseph and his brothers.

MOTHER: I have told you many times.

MIRIAM: I know, but it makes my heart happy to hear how God worked for the Hebrews.

MOTHER: Are you sure no one's outside?

MIRIAM: I will look again. (*Goes to window, returns.*) No, there is no one.

MOTHER: It was so long ago—four hundred years. We weren't always slaves and we weren't always afraid. We were a proud people, but famine came into our land.

MIRIAM: Tell me about Joseph and his brothers—how they sold him.

MOTHER: Joseph's brothers were jealous of him, and they sold him to some travelers who brought him to Egypt. But in all of his troubles he was faithful to Jehovah, even when they put him in prison. (*Stops after this; cocks head to one side as though listening; goes to window to look out.*)

MIRIAM: And while he was there in prison, God helped him to interpret Pharaoh's dream.

MOTHER (*returns to original place*): And Pharaoh raised him up to great honor and made him a ruler in Egypt. Then when the famine came Joseph's brothers came down to Egypt to buy grain.

MIRIAM: I wish our Pharaoh would have a dream and someone would explain it to him. Then maybe we'd get out of all this trouble.

MOTHER: Perhaps someday God will raise up a deliverer who will rescue us.

MIRIAM: And when Joseph's brothers came to Egypt, what happened?

MOTHER: Joseph gave them grain, and then, later he told them who he was, and all the family moved to Egypt.

MIRIAM: And Jehovah blessed our people, didn't He, Mother?

MOTHER: Yes, and we were fruitful and increased abundantly and multiplied, and we grew exceedingly mighty and the land was filled with us, and we were happy. But then—

MIRIAM: Then another Pharaoh came to power, and he didn't like us. And now look at all the trouble we have. Oh, baby brother, Pharaoh doesn't like you. Why doesn't God help us? Mother, is my baby brother going to be thrown into the river? (*Cries.*)

MOTHER: We can't hide him any more. He's three months old now. His voice is louder, and he is stronger. He needs to be in the sunshine, not hidden away in the darkness. But what will I do?

MIRIAM: Pharaoh's soldier's will find him and—

MOTHER (*moving quickly toward* MIRIAM): Wait! Hush! I have an idea.

MIRIAM: What?

Baby Moses 75

MOTHER: No one would think of looking for a LIVE baby in the river.
MIRIAM: What do you mean?
MOTHER: Perhaps we could hide him down there.
MIRIAM: How?
MOTHER: Then he'd be out in the fresh air, and away from the houses, and no one could hear him if he cried.
MIRIAM: But how could you hide him in the river?
MOTHER (*walks over to basket*): Look, we could put him in the basket and hide it in the reeds at the river's edge.
MIRIAM: But it would leak. He'd drown.
MOTHER: We could cover the basket with pitch. (*Bends over and picks basket up.*) We could make it waterproof, and it would be a little boat. The baby would be safe. We'd hide it in the reeds.
MIRIAM: But who would watch him? Who would take care of him?
MOTHER: You could stay near, at the water's edge. No one would pay any attention to you, and you could watch the baby.
MIRIAM: Oh, let's try it!
(*Curtain closes, remove window from back screen.*)

(SCENE TWO: *Curtain opens to show reeds and palm tree, basket in reeds, with baby in it.*)

MIRIAM (*bending over the basket and making motions, touching it, adjusting blanket, etc.; fig. 7g*): Now you are all right, baby brother. You're safely hidden. No one will harm you. That is a nice little boat you have. Go to sleep now, baby brother. (*Begins to hum.*)
PHARAOH'S DAUGHTER (*offstage*): It is very hot today.
MIRIAM: Hush, baby brother. I hear someone coming. (*Runs a distance and hides in other reeds.*)
PHARAOH'S DAUGHTER (*enters*): It has been hot today. I will

bathe in the river. Yes, we have had a long walk, and I am weary. The river will be nice—but—what is that? (*Points to basket.*) I see something in the river. Maid, go get that thing for me, I want to see what it is.

(MAID *moves toward basket.* MIRIAM *crouches down to try to hide herself.* MAID *picks up basket and brings it to* PHARAOH'S DAUGHTER, *hands it to her and bows, steps back a few feet.* PHARAOH'S DAUGHTER *puts basket on ground, opens the blanket.*)

PHARAOH'S DAUGHTER: Why, there's a baby here. What a cute little baby.

(MAID *approaches and looks in basket, turns back the blanket; baby begins to cry softly.*)

PHARAOH'S DAUGHTER: It's a little baby boy! Oh, don't cry, little one. This must be one of the Hebrew children. Oh, he is so sweet. (*Baby's cries increase.*) Don't cry, little one. (*Picks up the baby.*) No one will harm YOU. You poor little thing! I think I shall keep you for my very own son. But I need someone to feed you and care for you.

(MIRIAM *approaches; baby's cries fade to soft.*)

PHARAOH'S DAUGHTER: Yes, you are a sweet baby, but I need a nurse to care for you.

MIRIAM: Long life to you, daughter of the Pharaoh. Long life to you. Would you like me to call someone to care for your son? I could call one of the Hebrew women. She would nurse the baby for you.

PHARAOH'S DAUGHTER: Yes, call a nurse for me. Call one of the of the Hebrew women. I shall raise this baby as my own son.

(MIRIAM *leaves.* PHARAOH'S DAUGHTER *rocks baby back and forth; the cries stop.* MIRIAM *and* MOTHER *enter, both approach* PHARAOH'S DAUGHTER, *and bow.*)

MIRIAM: Long life to you, daughter of the Pharaoh. I have brought a Hebrew woman. She will nurse the child for you. (*Bows.*)

Baby Moses

PHARAOH'S DAUGHTER (*hands baby to* MOTHER): Take this child and nurse it for me, and I will pay you wages. He will be my son. No harm shall come to him. (*Pauses.*) Now, let's see. The child must have a name. What shall I call him? Oh, I know! I will call him Moses because I drew him out of the water. Take good care of Moses for me. I leave you now.

(MOTHER *and* MIRIAM *bow.* PHARAOH'S DAUGHTER *and* MAID *leave stage.*)

MIRIAM: Mother! We've got our baby back! He's safe!

MOTHER: Jehovah be thanked. Jehovah be praised. He has remembered His ancient people. He has heard my prayers.

(*Curtain closes.*)

78   *You Can Be a Puppeteer!*

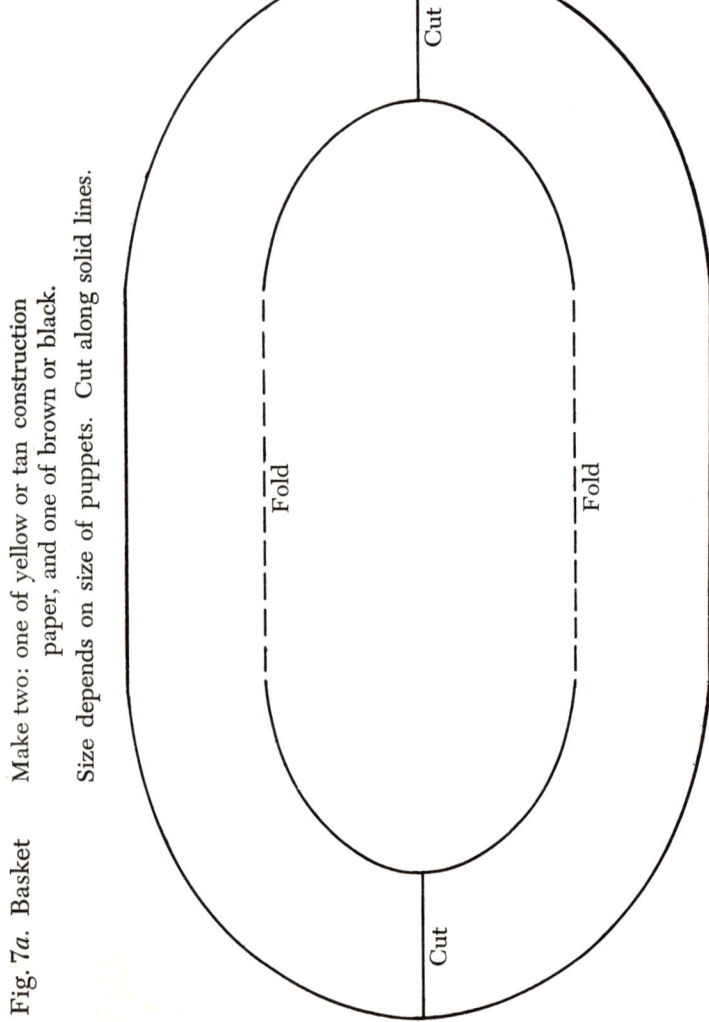

Fig. 7a. Basket   Make two: one of yellow or tan construction paper, and one of brown or black. Size depends on size of puppets. Cut along solid lines.

Staple or tape ends together.

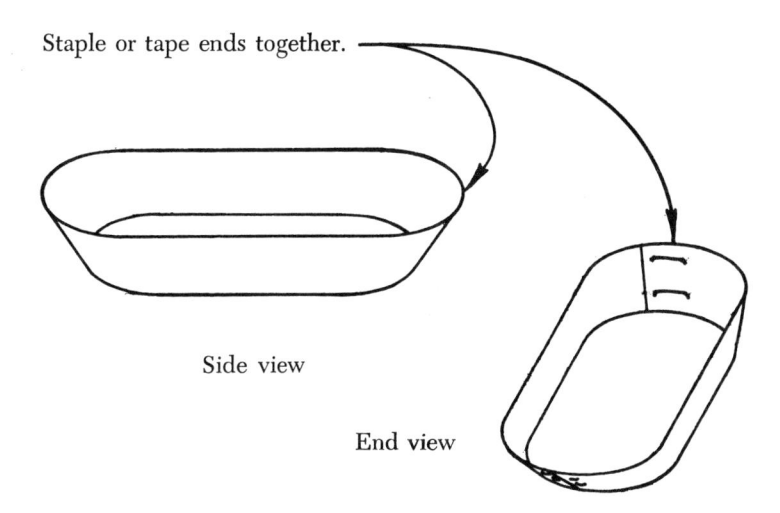

Side view

End view

Fig. 7b. Reeds

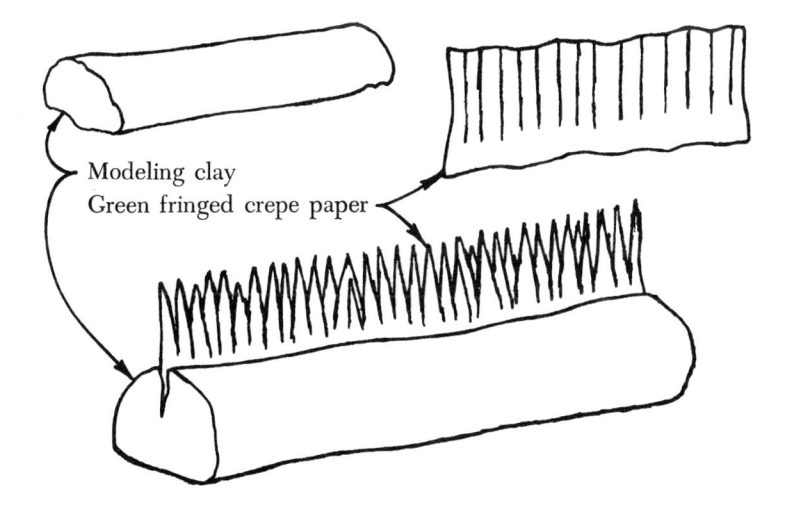

Modeling clay
Green fringed crepe paper

80 *You Can Be a Puppeteer!*

Fig. 7c. Stage for Scene One

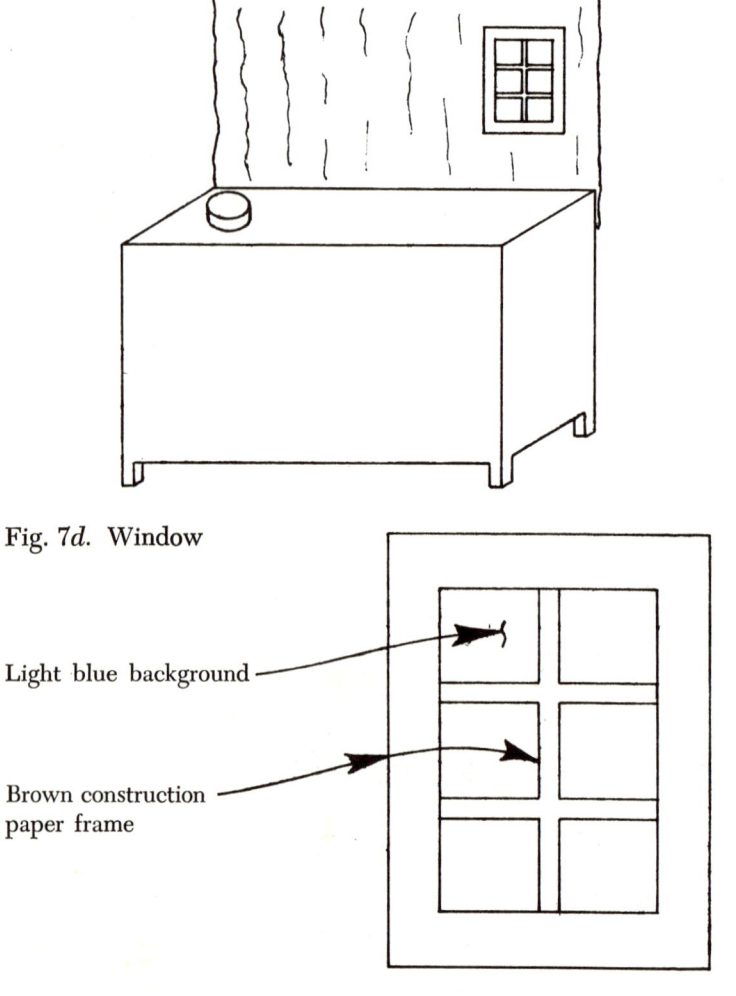

Fig. 7d. Window

Light blue background

Brown construction paper frame

Baby Moses 81

Figs. 7e-7f. Costumes

Gold paper cone

Pins

PHARAOH'S DAUGHTER

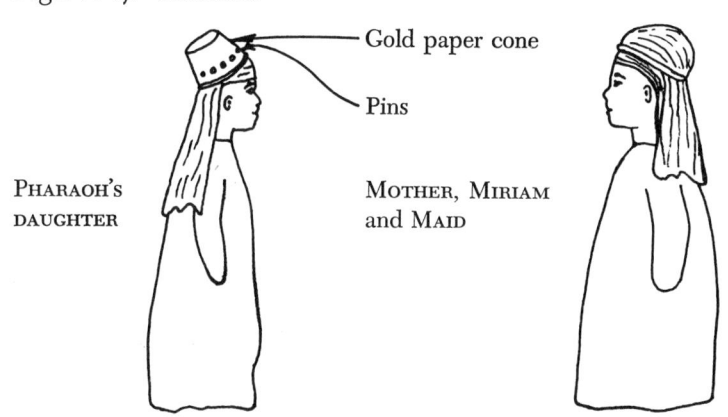

MOTHER, MIRIAM and MAID

Fig. 7g. Stage for Scene Two

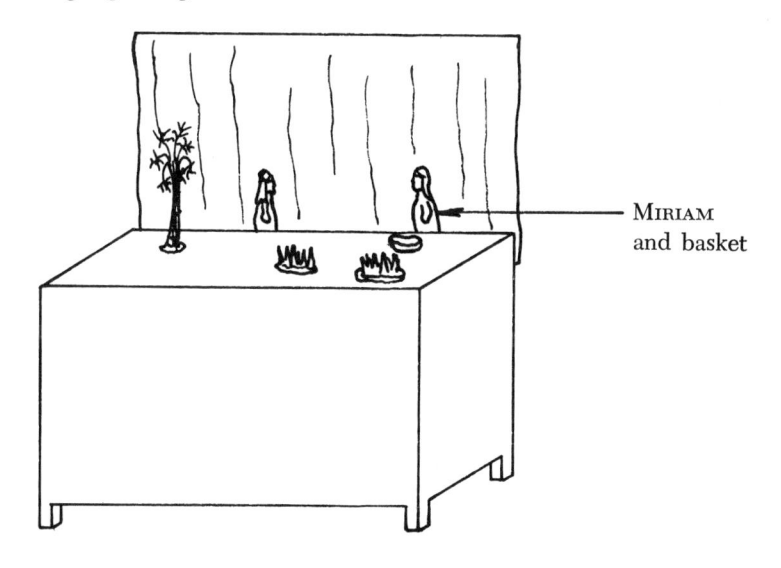

MIRIAM and basket

8

Elisha and the Widow's Oil

Puppet Play for Two Performers

Characters

| Elisha
1st son | First performer |
| Widow
2nd son | Second performer |

Props

Empty oil jars: These can be any type of container: empty pill jars colored brown, silver, black, and gold; clay pots; etc.

One filled jar of oil with oil pouring out: This should be smaller and different in shape and color from the empty ones. The oil is made by either cutting a stream of oil out of light brown shiny paper (colored part of a glossy magazine ad) or by stiffening light brown embroidery thread with clear nail polish and inserting it in the small jar (figs. 8a and 8b).

Window: See instructions for Window in chap. 7.

(SCENE ONE: *Curtains open to find* Elisha *on stage, pacing up and down.* Widow *enters.*)

Elisha: Greetings, woman. Have you come to see me?

Elisha and the Widow's Oil

WIDOW: Oh, yes, prophet Elisha. I have come to see you. I have great sorrow and much trouble.

ELISHA: I am sorry to hear that. Tell me, what has happened to make your heart sad?

WIDOW: Oh, Elisha, prophet of the Lord, my good husband has died.

ELISHA: I am sorry. Your husband was a good man.

WIDOW: Yes, Elisha, he was a follower of the Lord as you are, a prophet of the great God. But now he is dead, and I have great trouble.

ELISHA: Tell me, what is your problem?

WIDOW: I have nothing. No money. I owe much money. I have many debts, and I don't know what to do. Oh, I have great trouble.

ELISHA: Tell me what the trouble is.

WIDOW: I have two young sons, and now, because I cannot pay my debts, the men to whom I owe the money—they—they— (*Cries.*)

ELISHA: What is it that they are going to do?

WIDOW: Oh, sir, great prophet of the living God, they are going to take my two sons and sell them for slaves. Please sir, help me. Save my sons for me. Oh, if I only had money to pay my debts. Help me!

ELISHA: What shall I do for you? Tell me, what do you have in your house?

WIDOW: I don't have anything—nothing at all. Everything is gone except for one pot of oil. That's all I have, just one pot of oil. (*Cries.*)

ELISHA: Very well. Now go home, and borrow all the empty pots and jars that you can. Borrow a lot of them from all your neighbors, and when you have borrowed them, close your door and pour oil into these pots and set aside the full jars.

84   *You Can Be a Puppeteer!*

Widow: Yes, Elisha, I will do as you say.
(*Curtain closes.*)

(SCENE TWO: *Curtains open to find* Widow, 1st son, *and* 2nd son *inside house.*)

1st son: Mother, was the prophet Elisha able to help you?
2nd son: Are we going to be sold for slaves? Mother, I—I don't want to be a slave. I want to stay here with you.
Widow: Boys, Elisha has told me something very strange, and I do not understand it all. But I shall do as he has told me.
1st son: What did he say?
Widow: He said that I am to borrow all the empty jars that I can. Now hurry. Go out to the neighbors and bring all the jars you can. We must do as he says.
2nd son: What does he want them for?
Widow: I am to fill them with oil.
1st son: Where are you going to get the oil?
Widow: I am not sure, but—but I have a strange feeling that we are going to see something wonderful. Now hurry.
(Sons *leave.*)
Widow: Oh, I do not understand all the words that Elisha told me. But I will do everything he says. I must do these things to save my sons.
1st son (*returns with one pot*) Here is a big jar, Mother. Is this enough?
Widow: No, go get more, lots more. Now hurry.
2nd son (*enters with pot*). Here's a jar. Do you want more?
Widow: Yes, hurry. Borrow all you can find.
(Sons *put pots down and hurry out; they return with others; each time they enter,* Widow *tells them to get more;* Sons *keep running in bringing jars; finally the stage is full.*)
1st son (*enters huffing and puffing*): I—I have brought the last jar I could find. I ran all the way with it.
2nd son (*enters with jar*): This is the last one I can find.

Elisha and the Widow's Oil   85

WIDOW: Now I shall fill them with oil. I will go get my jar of oil. (*Leaves stage and returns with jar of oil. Her back can be kept toward the audience as she reenters so that they do not see the "oil" sticking up out of the pot. She moves to one jar and begins to pour. As she pours she turns slightly so that the audience can see the "oil" pouring out. Be sure not to tip the jar too far so that the oil will fall out too soon. If the oil is made out of paper and glued into the pot, it must be pulled out when the last jar is full. This is done by having the son who is holding the last jar, grab the paper along with the jar and pull it out. The "oil" can be dropped backstage as he moves the pot of oil.*)

1ST SON: How can you fill all these big jars from that little one?

2ND SON: There isn't enough oil in that jar to fill a big one.

WIDOW: Bring me a jar.

1ST SON: Here's one. (*Picks one up and carries it to* WIDOW; *she pours, and* SON *looks into jar.*) It's filling up. Quick, brother, bring more jars!

2ND SON (*runs up with jar*): Here. Oh, look! Look! This one is full too. (*Slips his jar under "stream" of oil.*)

1ST SON (*sets his jar down and picks up another and runs back to* WIDOW, *who continues pouring.*)

WIDOW: Look, God is working a miracle.

1ST SON: Mother, I can't believe it! The jars are being filled up.

2ND SON: And we just had one little bottle to begin with!

1ST SON: Here's another jar. It's—it's a miracle! (*They continue bringing jars and exclaiming until the last jar.*)

WIDOW: Quick, bring another jar.

1ST SON: This is the last one, Mother. There isn't another empty one.

WIDOW: Look again. Find another. There is still more oil.

2ND SON (*looks into jars*): They are all full.

1ST SON: This jar is full now, too. (*Tip the small jar up so that the stream of oil falls into the last jar; or grab the paper stream of oil with* 1st son's *hands, as he holds the jar, and pull the "oil" out of small jar. Drop backstage as he moves with jar of oil.*)

Widow: Look, the oil has stopped pouring. God has worked a miracle! Our jars are full. How wonderful! Now I've got to go and find Elisha, and see what he wants me to do. (*Leaves.*)

Sons (*both examine full pots*).

1st son: It's a miracle!

2nd son: All the pots are full!

1st son: I've never seen so much oil. I didn't know there was this much oil in the world.

2nd son: God has blessed us. He is a good God, and I thank Him.

Widow (*reenters*): Sons, the prophet Elisha has said that we must sell the oil and then we will have enough money to pay our debts.

1st son: We won't have to be slaves?

2nd son: We can stay with you?

Widow: Yes, God has worked a miracle. We are saved! I will sell the oil, and what is left over after paying the debts, the prophet Elisha says we can have to live on., Oh, God has truly blessed us.

1st son: He is a good God.

2nd son: He has saved us. He has taken care of us!

(Sons *jump up and down with joy and clap their hands.*)

1st son: We are saved!

Widow: Let's tell Him we are thankful. Let's tell Him we are grateful to Him.

(*All bow heads, hands held together as in prayer. Curtain closes.*)

Elisha and the Widow's Oil 87

Figs. 8a-8b. Jar with oil pouring out

8a

Oil: piece of shiny, light brown paper

or

8b

Tan embroidery thread stiffened with clear nail polish

9

Idol Breaker

(A Story from Africa)

PUPPET PLAY FOR TWO HANDS

CHARACTERS

FATHER: a maker of idols
IGWE: a student

PROPS

IDOLS (made of eggs): Choose several large, white eggs; wash thoroughly with cold water; dry. Pierce the smaller end with a very large darning needle. It is necessary to break the inner membrane around the uncooked egg. Pierce the larger end of the egg, and if needed, gently prick away a small amount of the shell, so that the opening is about ¼" wide. (It may be necessary to make the opening on the smaller end a bit larger. Be sure that the membrane on both ends of the egg is broken.) Now, holding the pierced egg over a cup or bowl, place your mouth over the smaller end, and blow hard. The egg will come out with the yolk broken.

Wash the blown eggshell under cold running water and set upright on paper towels to drain dry. Now paint the dried eggshells with poster (tempera) paints so that they resemble

Idol Breaker

grotesque faces (figs. 9a-9d). Some of the eggshells may be painted brown and left without faces to represent wooden forms not yet completed. Using papier-maché, clay, or plasticine, make bases for these egg "idols" so that they may stand upright. One of the "idols" should be on a higher base than the others. This is the Yam God (fig. 9d).

Ax: Take the lid from a small tin can, like a tomato puree or baby food can. Taking care not to cut your fingers, fold it over, so that it is double (fig. 9e). Now take a twig about six inches long, or a piece of doweling, and make a slit long enough for the tin to fit into. Slip a length of heavy duty thread, or very light wire through the folded lid (fig. 9f) and insert the lid into the slit. Now wrap the wire or thread around the slit to hold it together and to hold the lid in place (fig. 9g).

Costuming

The characters may wear simple white gowns. Also, a string of colorful beads can be made from old costume jewelry.

(SCENE ONE: *Curtain opens to find* FATHER *with ax in hand working on one of the idols. The idols are in a row along the stage with the Yam God at one end of the row.* FATHER *merely taps the idol to appear that he is working on it.*)

FATHER (*puts a few finishing touches on idol, steps back*): There! That idol is finished. But where is my lazy son Igwe? He should have been here a long time ago to help with this work. Sometimes I am very sorry I let him go to that mission school. His head is full of nonsense. And he keeps talking about this one called Jesus. He has made me feel very unhappy lately. I wish he'd come. I have a lot of work for him to do.

IGWE (*enters, bows to* FATHER): Greetings, Father.

You Can Be a Puppeteer!

FATHER (*drops ax, hurries over to* IGWE, *and hits him over the head with hand.* IGWE *ducks, hides head in hands*): You! Where have you been? You are a lazy son, and you don't care about me anymore. (*Hits* IGWE *again.*)

IGWE: Father! Please don't hit me. I—I—

FATHER (*hitting* IGWE): You are lazy. You were supposed to come home and work on these idols. We have much work to do.

IGWE: Father, I stayed after school. I just came from there. (*Points in direction he has just entered.*)

FATHER: And what did you have to stay after school for? I suppose that you have done something wrong. Nothing is right anymore. I can't sleep. I'm not happy. I keep thinking about the things you have told me about Jesus. I think the gods are angry with us. Never have I felt so unhappy. (*Turns and walks back to the Yam God, bows low.*) Oh, Yam God, hear my prayers; give me peace and happiness. Make my son be a good boy to me, his old father. Hear my prayer, oh, hear my prayer.

IGWE (*covers ears with hands*): Father, that Yam God can't hear you. His ears are just painted.

FATHER (*rushes back to* IGWE *and hits him*): The Yam God is angry because you talk this way. (*Leans over and picks up the ax; works on one of the gods for a minute.*) I have much work to do. Get busy and help me. You have not told me why you stayed after school.

IGWE: I stayed after school and talked to the missionary about Jesus.

FATHER (*throws the ax down again; turns angrily to* IGWE): Stop! I will not have you talk about this Jesus anymore! Do you want the gods to rise up and kill us all? I think I shall take you out of school.

IGWE: Oh, no, Father, not that.

FATHER: The only reason I let you go to school was so that you

Idol Breaker

could learn to read and write to help me keep accounts. But you are lazy. You won't work here in my shop helping me to make new idols. Always you are talking about this one called Jesus. Ha! I have had enough of this. Get busy and work! You are not good.

IGWE: Father, I want to be a good son to you.

FATHER: The spirits are angry with me. I toss and I turn. My heart is full of sorrow. The gods are angry.

IGWE: Father, they are made of wood! They cannot hear—

FATHER: Stop! Do you want the spirits to hear you? Do you want the gods to kill you?

IGWE: Father, today I learned something out of the Bible. That is what I stayed after school for.

FATHER: This school has filled your head with nonsense.

IGWE: Father, you are Wuku, the greatest of the idol makers, and I am your son. I want to obey you. (*Points to* FATHER.) But my heart (*hand on heart*) is torn between two things. (*Points to* FATHER *and then towards heaven.*) Father, the Bible says, "Their idols are silver and gold, the work of men's hands. They have mouths, but they speak not; eyes have they, but they see not: They have ears, but they hear not: noses have they, but they smell not: They have hands, but they handle not: feet have they, but they walk not: neither speak they through their throats."

FATHER (*runs over and tries to stop* IGWE's *mouth with his hand*): Stop it! Do not talk that way. The gods will be angry. I am afraid! Oh, I am afraid!

IGWE (*points to idols*): You're always afraid of them. But they do not help you or make you happy. You always say that they must have more grain and other sacrifices. But they are no good!

FATHER (*bows head and covers head with hands*): You are speaking foolishly.

IGWE: Father, the missionary says that Jesus is the true God.

He hears our prayers. I do not want to be afraid and follow these wooden things. I want to trust in Jesus. He is the true God.

FATHER (*hits* IGWE): The gods will punish us. I must go and get more grain and make a sacrifice to them. (*runs out of room.*)

IGWE (*sobs; make* IGWE *"cry" by covering face with hands, bowing over slightly and shaking "shoulders"*): Those horrid old idols. They are no good! (*Looks around and picks up ax.*) I wonder if they can do anything. (*Touches one god with ax.*) Hey, you, you wooden god. Can you hear me? Huh? Can you hear me. If you can hear me, stop me. Stop me if you can. You have frightened my father for many years. You have made him unhappy. I don't think you can hear me. Go on, kill me if you can. Go on, kill me. But quit making my father afraid. (*Touches ax harder to the idol.*)

I'm just a little boy, but kill me if you can, you old wooden idol. Go on, kill me. (*Hits idol harder.*) Kill me, but stop making my father afraid. (*Stops and looks at idol.*) Hah! it never moved. It didn't feel the ax. The Bible is right. The Bible tells the truth! The old idol can't hurt me. It can't hurt my father. It's just wood. (*Hits idol harder and smashes it.*) There! Take that, you funny old thing. (*Moves on to the next idol.*) There, kill me if you can, you funny old thing with the big nose. (*Stops, puts ax down and covers eyes.*) This is the idol that my father says can cause me to be blind. I–I (*Voice sounds fearful.*) I'm afraid. (*Moves one hand.*) I can still see. I'm not blind. I'm not dead. Nothing has happened! I'm alive! They aren't gods. They are just wood. They can't feel or see or hear. (*Begins to smash all idols except the Yam God.*) There! Take that, you silly old piece of wood. There, now you are dead. Take that, and that and that. (*Laughs and shouts.*) You're just wood! You aren't

Idol Breaker

really gods at all. Jesus is the true God. You're just wood! Please help me, Jesus, help me! (*Pauses.*)

Now I know what I'll do. I'll just put this ax down by the Yam God and I'll go to sleep. (*Lays ax down and lies down on floor, covers head with arms as though he is asleep.*)

FATHER (*enters after a few seconds; throws hands up over head in horror*): Igwe! Igwe! Are you dead? Oh, oh, oh. My son is dead! My idols have killed him!

IGWE (*sits up slowly, stretches; yawns*): Oh, Father, I was asleep! What's the matter?

FATHER: Matter? What has happened? Look! My idols—they are all ruined. Igwe! You—you did this! You destroyed my idols!

IGWE (*points hand to chest*): I? I destroy your idols? Father, how could I? I was asleep.

FATHER: Igwe, you destroyed my idols. (*Begins to hit* IGWE.)

IGWE (*dodging blows*): Father, look! Here is the ax. It is right by the Yam God. You see, FATHER, it was the Yam God. He killed the others.

FATHER (*hitting* IGWE): Don't be silly. Of course he didn't do it. He couldn't do it. He's just made out of wood. He can't do anything. You did it.

IGWE: You are right, Father. He IS just made out of wood. He couldn't do a thing. He couldn't help the other idols. I smashed them, and the Yam God didn't help them. So he can't help you, either.

FATHER (*holding head*): Oh, why have you ruined my idols?

IGWE: I did it for you, Father.

FATHER (*angrily hitting* IGWE): What do you mean, you did it for me?

IGWE: I didn't want you to be afraid of them. So I broke them up. I was afraid at first. I thought they might blind me or kill me. But I didn't want you to be afraid of them anymore. I want you to love Jesus and be happy. So I broke them up.

Jesus helped me. Father, you are known as the maker of idols. I will be known as the BREAKER of idols.

IGWE (*picks up ax and begins to hit the Yam God.* FATHER *tries to hold him back but isn't successful.* FATHER *puts hands over head and falls to ground, moaning in fear.*)

FATHER: We shall die! We shall die.

IGWE: No, look, Father. Look, the Yam God is dead!

FATHER (*peeks out from under one hand*): The Yam God is dead? He hasn't killed you—or me?

IGWE: No, Father, he can't hurt us. He is only a wooden idol. Jesus is the true and living God.

FATHER (*rising slowly*): Igwe, I don't understand this. My idols are all dead. They couldn't protect themselves. Igwe, they didn't protect themselves.

IGWE: Father, I think we should go talk to the missionary, don't you?

FATHER: Yes, Igwe, I want to learn about the one called Jesus who makes you brave enough to do this to help me. My idols are dead. I want to hear about the living God. (*Puts arm around* IGWE's *shoulder, they exit together. Curtain closes.*)

Idol Breaker

Figs. 9*a*-9*c*. Idols

9*a*

9*b*

9*c*

Fig. 9*d*. Yam God

96   *You Can Be a Puppeteer!*

Figs. 9*e*-9*g*. Making the ax

9*e*

wire

9*f*   Folded lid

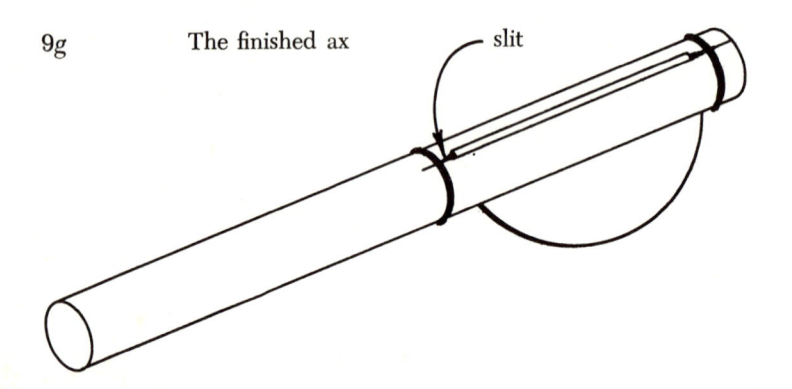

9*g*   The finished ax   slit

10

Pinata

PUPPET PLAY FOR FOUR HANDS

(A Christmas story, but could be for other times by using words in brackets)

CHARACTERS

PEPITO: small boy
CARLOS: smaller boy
FATHER: Mexican
MISSIONARY: American

PROPS

Bible
pinata
broom
water jug
stick to break pinata

cap (red and blue)
pencil (short stub)
piece of paper
small gifts in pinata

DIRECTIONS FOR MAKING PROPS

BIBLE: Cut a rectangle of black paper to be the cover of the Bible. The size depends on the size of your puppets; however, it does not need to be to scale with puppets, but large enough to be seen from audience, and easy for a puppet to hold, about 3½"x2½". Now cut several small pieces of white paper and place in the center of the black sheet. Stitch or staple together and fold down the middle (fig. 10*a*).

PINATA: This should be made out of a circle of tissue paper or Christmas wrapping paper and decorated with gold and silver stars. Make it into a pouch-shaped container, gathering the top together by either stapling or sewing it. Fasten ribbon to the top so that the pinata can be raised or lowered. Stick a hook or pin into the loop end of the ribbon so that it can be fastened in place. (See figs. 10*b*-10*e*.) A "floor" (a piece of cardboard tacked across from stage to back curtain) must be in place to keep the gifts from falling behind the scenes and being lost to sight. This should not take up more than one quarter of the usual working space on the stage, or the characters will not have room to move.

GIFTS: The pinata should be partially filled with small "gifts." These are just wads of colored paper tied to look like gifts. Something heavy like a washer or marble could be put inside them to make them fall easier.

BROOM: This may be made by tying a few short pieces of straw taken from a broom onto a twig, or heavy brown wrapping paper folded about four times and "fringed" may be tied onto a twig (fig. 10*f*).

WATER JUGS: These can be small plastic pill containers painted brown or red.

COSTUMING

Dress PEPITO in ragged clothes and CARLOS in good clothes, perhaps using ponchos. FATHER should be dressed as a Mexican and MISSIONARY as an American.

(SCENE ONE: *Keeping the scenery to a minimum, either use a background curtain painted to represent a Mexican house, white walls, red tile roof; or use a small cutout on the side of the stage to represent a house* (fig. 10*g*). *The pinata is fastened to the back curtain by means of a hook and/or pins, and ar-*

Pinata

ranged so that it can be let down like a bucket is lowered into a well, so that Pepito *can place the cap in it, and* Carlos *can put the piece of paper in. Curtain opens to find* Carlos *reading the Bible.* Pepito *enters carrying water jug. He moves across stage and looks over* Carlos' *shoulder and splatters a bit of water.*)

Carlos (*jumps up and moves away*): I hate you, Pepito. I hate you! Look what you did! You spilled water on my new shirt.

Pepito: Carlos! I am sorry. I only wanted to look over your shoulder and see what it was that you were reading. I am sorry, Carlos. Forgive me. (*Carries water to one side and sets the jug down.*)

Carlos: I will tell my father to beat you, Pepito. Look, you even got water on my Bible!

Pepito: I am sorry, Senor Carlos, I am sorry. Forgive me. Ah, it would be so good to be able to read.

Carlos: You are very clumsy, Pepito. It is a wonder that you do not drown yourself when you get water from the river. It is a wonder that you do not break my mama's waterpots, and you are slow.

Pepito: I am a good water carrier. I do not break the waterpots, and I do not waste time.

Carlos: Si, that is what my papa is always telling me. He says, "Why don't you work hard like Pepito does? Why aren't you polite like Pepito?" Ah, I am sick of hearing about you. Go away. Leave me alone. You would not be able to read this Book anyway. Only those who have been to school can read. You are too stupid.

Pepito: I am sorry, Carlos. I did not mean to splatter water. It is a nice shirt too, but it will dry. Next year I will learn to read. My mama says that next year, if I work hard and we can save any money, I can go to school. Now much of my money is for my papa's medicine. He is very sick. Someday I will go to school and learn to read. Then I can read the sacred Book for myself. Oh, Carlos, it will be good to learn to read the Bible. Every Sunday when I go to the mission I listen to Senor Missionary tell about Jesus. Someday I will read the Bible and learn all about Him.

FATHER (*enters while* PEPITO *is talking*): Good boy, Pepito. I see that you have filled our water jars. Now this is Christmas Eve [my birthday], and it would be good if you would join our family for the fiesta tonight. We will have a feast, and we will break the pinata.

CARLOS: But Papa—

PEPITO: Oh, senor, I thank you. I am happy—

CARLOS: But Papa—I—

FATHER: Carlos, I told you that you should sweep the veranda. You are lazy. You should be more like Pepito. He is a good boy.

CARLOS: Sweeping the veranda is woman's work. Let the servants do it! Or let Pepito; He is just a peasant.

FATHER (*slaps* CARLOS *angrily*): Do not speak that way. Pepito is your brother in Jesus. You must be kind to him. Now get busy. Everyone is busy. We have a special guest tonight. The missionary from the United States is coming to help us celebrate Christmas Eve [to celebrate with us].

CARLOS (*lays the Bible down, turns his back to* PEPITO, *picks up broom, and begins to sweep*): I am not happy.

PEPITO: It is a beautiful pinata, senor. I would be so happy to come. But—but if Carlos is angry—

FATHER: Carlos' anger will cool. You will come tonight for the feast and for the breaking of the pinata.

PEPITO: Thank you, muchas gracias, senor. Good-bye, Carlos, until this evening, adios.

FATHER: Adios, may God go with you.

PEPITO (*leaves*).

FATHER (*turning to* CARLOS): You should be kinder to Pepito.

Pinata

His father is very sick, and Pepito works very hard, and they are poor. (*Leaves.*)

CARLOS: I do not see why I have to do this work. This is no work for one who can read. I am sick of Pepito. Always Father is saying, "Be good like Pepito." Now he will come and perhaps he will break the pinata. It is not fair.
(*Curtain closes.*)

(SCENE TWO: *Curtain opens to find* MISSIONARY *and* CARLOS *in the same setting as Scene One.*)

MISSIONARY: Carlos, tell me about the pinata. In my country we do not have such a beautiful custom.

CARLOS: Oh, Senor Missionary, the pinata is full of beautiful gifts for everyone. There is also a gift for you, senor. My papa told me that there is a gift for you and—and—

MISSIONARY: And—what, Carlos?

CARLOS: He even put a gift in for Pepito!

MISSIONARY: It is nice that Pepito is coming to your fiesta.

CARLOS: He is taller than I, and I'm afraid that he will break the pinata. You know, it is our custom for each child to be given a chance to break the pinata. It is a great honor to break it and cause the gifts to fall to the ground.

MISSIONARY: I think that Pepito would enjoy that. His family is too poor to have a pinata. I have just come from his house. The only gift that Pepito will get this year is a cap. His mother has knitted it for him; it is red and blue. (*Pauses.*) You know, Carlos, the pinata reminds me of the Lord Jesus.

CARLOS: Huh? And how is that, Senor Missionary?

MISSIONARY: When Jesus died on the cross He poured out His life for us and gave us eternal life and forgiveness. He was broken, just like the pinata is broken. When you break the pinata, you get your lovely gifts. When the Lord Jesus died, His blood was shed for our sins so that we could have eternal life.

CARLOS: Ah, that is good, Senor Missionary.

MISSIONARY: Jesus poured out His love for us. He loved us when we were poor ragged beggars.

CARLOS: Ragged beggars, senor?

MISSIONARY: Si, Carlos. What did we have to offer the Lord Jesus? Nothing! But He loved us in spite of the fact that all we had was our poor sinful hearts.

CARLOS: I see, senor.

PEPITO (*enters with blue and red cap in hand*): Buenos dias, Senor Missionary. Greetings, Carlos. I have a small gift for you, Carlos. My mother said that I must not come empty-handed to your fiesta. Senor Missionary, if you would let down the pinata I would like to put my gift for Carlos into it.

(MISSIONARY *lowers pinata, and* PEPITO *places cap in it.* MISSIONARY *starts to bring it up, but* CARLOS *stops him.*)

CARLOS: Wait, Senor Missionary. I, too, have a gift. (*Picks up pencil and looks for paper.*) Now where is that paper? Oh, here it is. (*Writes.*) Now, Senor missionary, put this paper in the pinata, too. It is a gift for Pepito.

FATHER (*enters*): Welcome! Now it is time to break the pinata. Carlos, you are the smallest child, would you like to begin?

CARLOS: No, Father, let our guest, Pepito, begin. Here, Pepito, take this stick and strike the pinata. (*Picks up stick and hands it to* PEPITO.)

PEPITO: Gracias, thank you, Carlos. (*Swings the stick, missing the pinata.*)

CARLOS: Try again.

PEPITO (*swings, breaks the pinata, gifts fall to the ground*): Oh, the marvelous gifts! How pretty!

CARLOS: Thank you for the cap, Pepito. (*Goes over to the paper and picks it up.*) This is your gift. I will read it to you. (*Reads.*) "Dear Pepito, you were generous to bring the beautiful cap that your mother made for you, so I will give

Pinata

you a gift. Every day, when you bring water, I will teach you some reading. Next year, when you go to school you will already know much reading. This is my gift to you."

PEPITO *and* CARLOS (*throw arms around each other*): This is a good Christmas [fiesta]. Thank you!

(*Curtain closes.*)

Fig. 10a. Bible

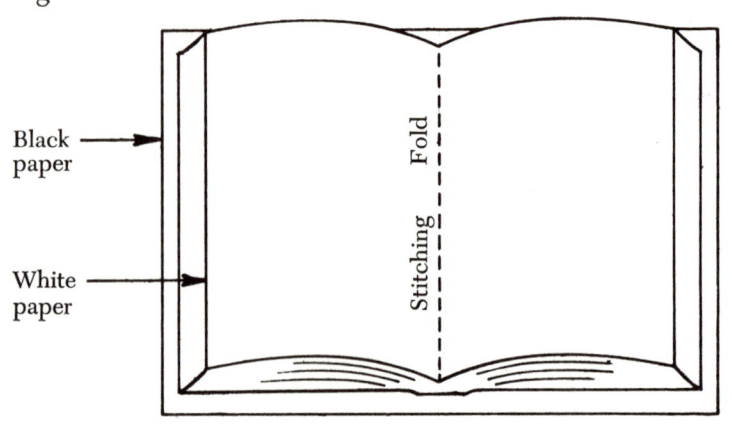

Black paper →

White paper →

Stitching | Fold

Figs. 10b-d. Making the pinata

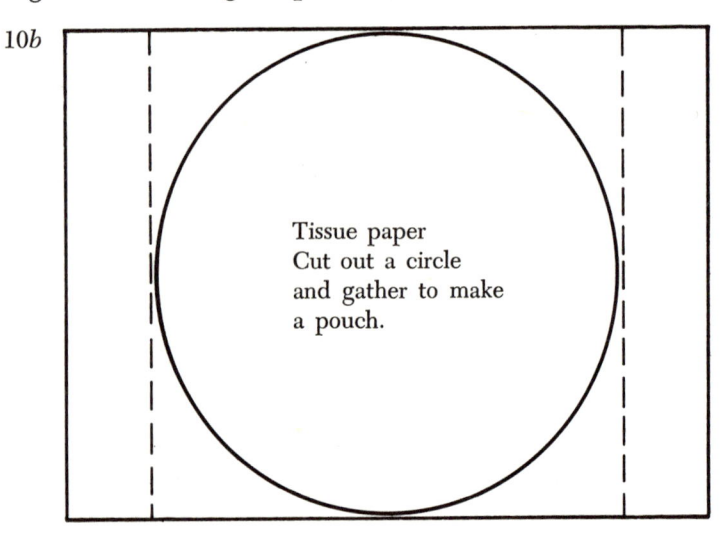

10b

Tissue paper
Cut out a circle
and gather to make
a pouch.

Pinata 105

10c

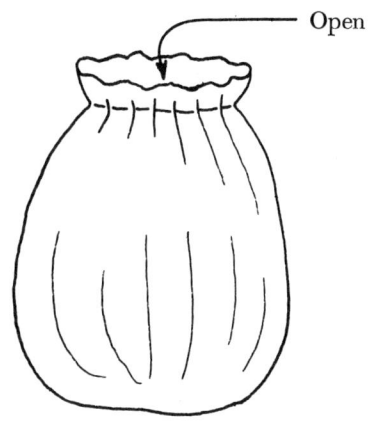

Stitching or staples
to hold gathers

Open

10d

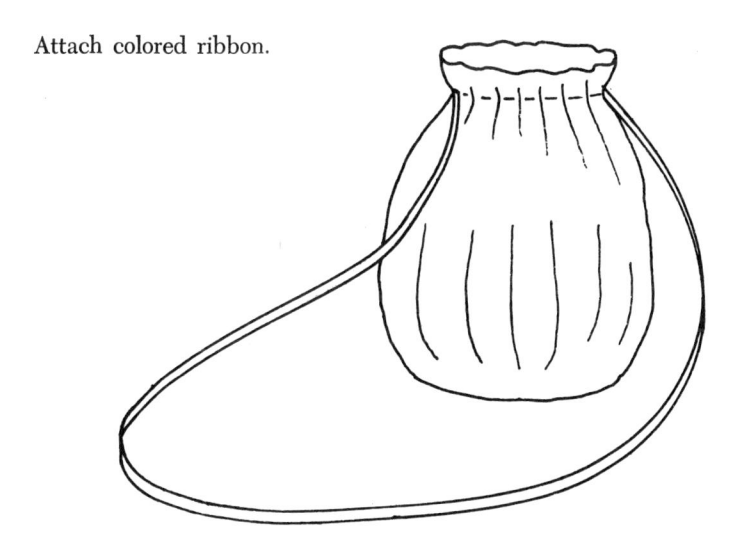

Attach colored ribbon.

Fig. 10e. Stage for Scene Two

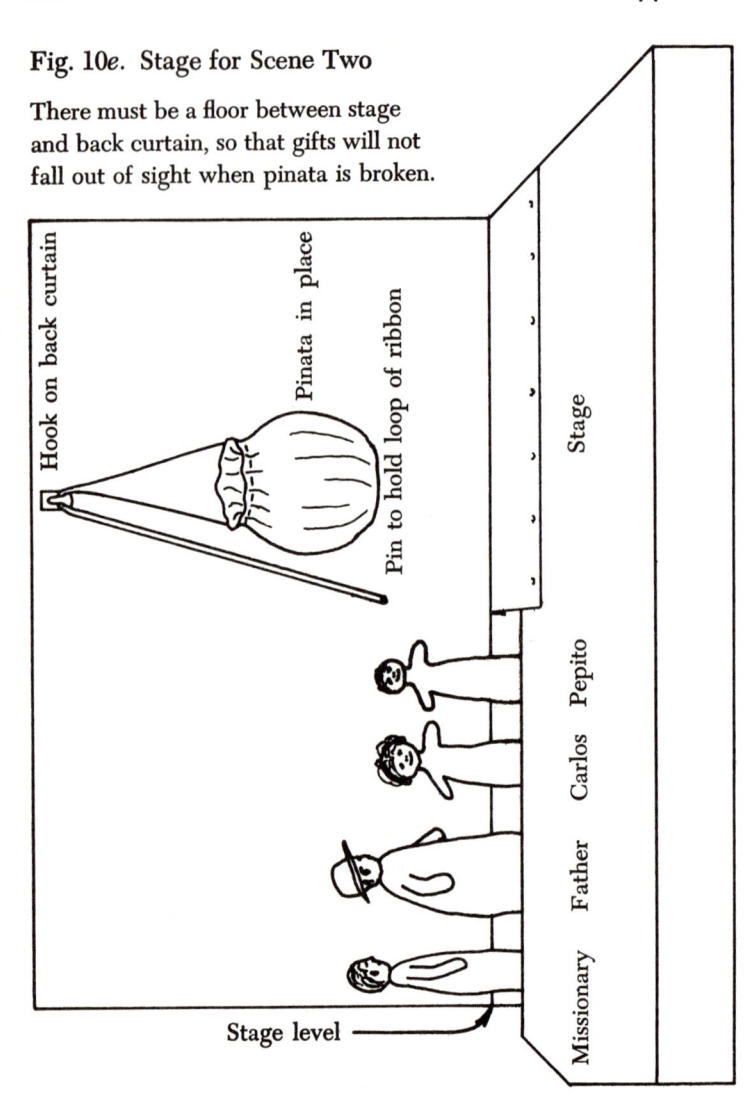

There must be a floor between stage and back curtain, so that gifts will not fall out of sight when pinata is broken.

Pinata 107

Fig. 10*f*. Broom

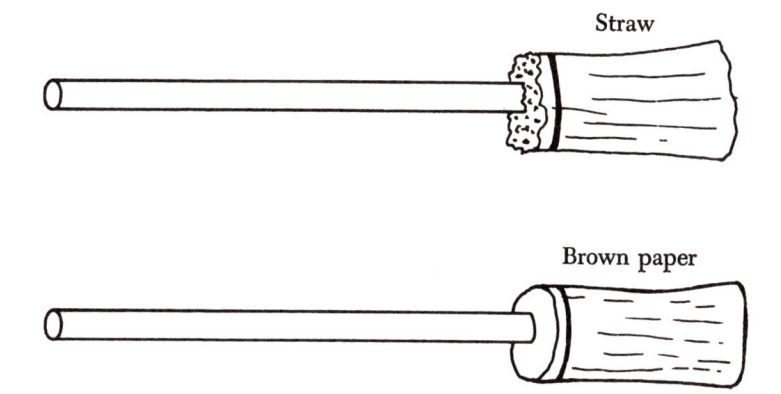

Straw

Brown paper

Fig. 10*g*. Stage

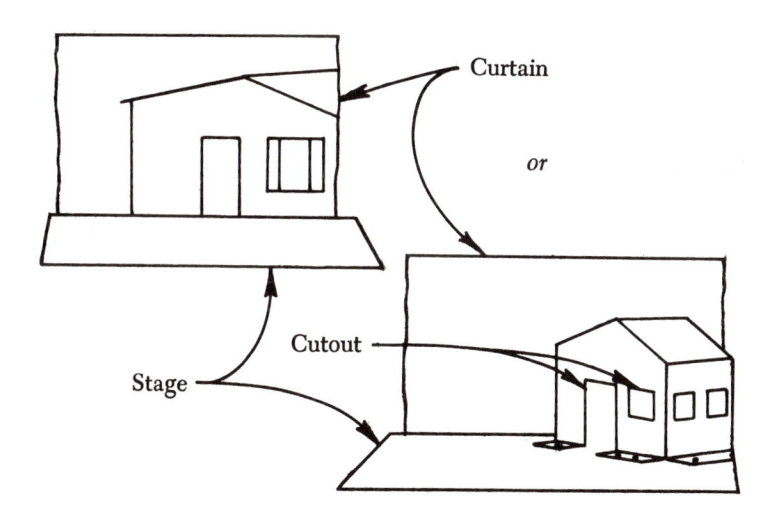

Curtain

or

Cutout

Stage

11

Wong Lee's Mystery Box

(A Missionary Story from China)

Characters

WONG LEE: Chinese boy
FATHER: Chinese man

Props

small red bird on thin black thread
small box with hinged lid
small hoe
tree

Directions for Making Props

RED BIRD: Use a small toy bird or cut a small bird out of red construction paper. Thin black thread is fastened to the bird's back and bird is placed in box, thread hanging out. For Scene Two, use needle to pull thread through tree top and backdrop (fig. 11c).

Box WITH LID: To make, use pattern (fig. 11a) and cut from construction paper. Box is fastened by simple hook and loop made out of light wire (fig. 11b).

HOE: This is made by folding a small piece of heavy aluminum foil and inserting it in slit end of a small twig (fig. 11d).

Wong Lee's Mystery Box

TREE: This may be cut from green and brown felt and attached to backdrop, or drawn on back curtain.

(SCENE ONE: *Tree is to one side of the stage. Curtain opens to find* WONG LEE *with hoe over shoulder. He takes hoe from shoulder and makes a few motions as though he is hoeing.*)

WONG LEE (*grumbling*): I do not see why I must work all the time. I wish I had all the money in the world, then I would never work. My father says that Adam sinned, and that caused the world to be punished. I would never have been stupid like old Adam. I hate work. (*Throws hoe down and lies down.*) I will just lie here and rest for a few minutes. It is not right that I should have to work.

FATHER (*enters*): Wong Lee, I told you to work in the garden.

WONG LEE: Honorable Father, I am tired of working.

FATHER: I do not think you have worked hard enough to be tired. I see no sign of the garden having been worked on at all.

WONG LEE: But I am tired. I don't like to work. I don't like to go to school. I don't like—

FATHER: You don't like a lot of things. I am tired of your grumbling all the time. You are lazy.

WONG LEE: But you said it was Adam's fault that the earth was cursed. I don't see why I have to work just because Adam was foolish and sinned.

FATHER: Do you remember what the missionary told us? He said that sin caused all our grief and sorrows. But we must work now, and you too must work. You cannot blame Adam for all your troubles.

WONG LEE: I am a good boy. I wouldn't do anything foolish like Adam did when he disobeyed God.

FATHER: We are all sinners. We have all disobeyed God. The Bible tells us that there is none righteous.

WONG LEE: I'M righteous.

FATHER: You are a grumbler. Now get to work on the garden, and then hurry off to school. (*Leaves.*)

WONG LEE (*picks up hoe, makes a couple moves with it; throws it down and sits down*): I shall rest a bit before I begin to work. (*Slowly* WONG LEE's *head begins to nod and he falls asleep.*) (*Curtain closes.*)

(SCENE TWO: *Curtain opens to find* WONG LEE *still asleep.* FATHER *stands nearby; box with bird inside is located wherever puppeteer can make it work correctly. Thread is extended through tree top to other side where puppeteer can pull it easily.*)

WONG LEE (*wakes up, stretches, then sees* FATHER): Oh, Honorable Father, I was just resting before I begin work.

FATHER: You do not need to work now, my son.

WONG LEE: Not need to work, Honorable Father? What happened?

FATHER: Nothing. I just do not want you to work anymore. From now on, anything you want to do, you may do.

WONG LEE: You are talking to me, Father?

FATHER: Yes, my son, you need never work again. You do not need to go to school, either.

WONG LEE: Honorable Father speaks words that I do not understand.

FATHER: Honorable Father speaks the truth. Never need you work. Only, one thing—

WONG LEE: I THOUGHT Honorable Father was joking.

FATHER: No joke. Only one thing. You see this little box? Do not touch this box. When you open it, back you go to work, and back you go to school.

WONG LEE (*jumps up, moves toward box, puts hand out as though to touch it*): What's in it, Father?

FATHER: No! Do not touch it. The moment you touch that box, back you go to work, back you go to school. You may

Wong Lee's Mystery Box

do anything you want—forever, but you do not touch that box.

WONG LEE: I do not care about the box! You mean, I can eat all I want and play all I want?

FATHER: Yes, only do not touch that box! I leave you now. Enjoy yourself.

WONG LEE: Oh, Honorable Father, thank you.

(FATHER *leaves.*)

WONG LEE: This is Honorable Wong Lee's lucky day! No more work! No more school! (*Jumps up and begins to dance.*) I am happy! No more work! (*Claps hands.*) No more school! All the food I want to eat! All the sleep I want to sleep. (*Stops suddenly.*) I wonder what is in the box? But—who cares? The box is no interest to me. (*Pauses.*) It is a strange-looking box. (*All the time* WONG LEE *gradually moves nearer to the box, then moves back a couple of steps, then forward three, until at the end of the following monolog he is at the box.*)

Father said that Adam sinned, and that all of us are sinners, but I will not do anything as foolish as Adam did. I do not care to touch something that is forbidden. I wonder what's in the box? Never mind! I think I will go to the river and swim. But (*pauses*), I wonder, what is in that box? Oh, well, I won't even look at it (*pauses*), but it is such a strange-looking box. I never saw a box like that before. I wonder where my father got it. It won't hurt to look at it. (*Kneels by box.*) I think I hear something inside the box. (*Places ear on box.*) Yes, there is something moving inside. I wonder what it is. (*Looks all around.*) Father is nowhere around. I will just take a quick peek inside. (*Opens box. Bird "flies" out—pull on thread in back of curtain.*)

Ooooh! (*Falls back in fright.*) A bird. Oh, bird! Bird, come back! (*Tries to catch bird. Bird flies out of his way—*

pull bird up to tree top.) Oh, bird, come back. Bird come back. (*Tries to catch bird and fails.*)

FATHER (*enters angrily*): Well, Wong Lee, I see that you have disobeyed me.

WONG LEE (*hangs head*): Oh, Father, I am sorry. I just wanted to see what was in the box.

FATHER: And now you know. And now you go back to work.

WONG LEE: Yes, Father, I am sorry.

FATHER: Now you know that you have done the same thing that Adam did. You see, Wong Lee, it is as the missionary told us. We are all sinners.

WONG LEE: Yes, Father, I understand. You put the bird in the box to show me that I couldn't obey. I am sorry. I will try to be a better son.

FATHER: Wong Lee, the little bird is red. Red is the color of blood. What does that remind you of?

WONG LEE: It reminds me of the blood of the Lord Jesus. I will ask Jesus to forgive me and make me a good boy. (*They bow their heads.*) Dear Jesus, thank You for dying for me. Thank You for shedding your blood for me. Help me to be a good boy. Amen. (*Looks up to* FATHER.) Father, I think that every time I see a red bird I will remember this day. I am glad that Jesus died for me.

(*Curtain closes.*)

Wong Lee's Mystery Box 113

Figs. 11a-11b. Box with lid

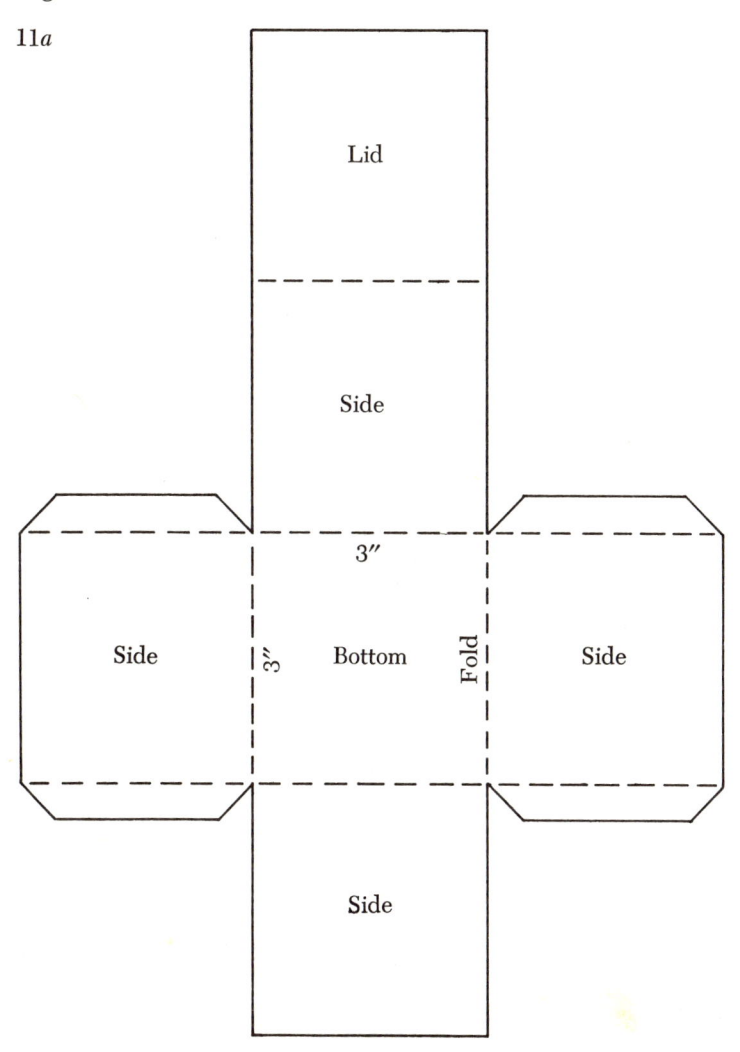

11a

Lid

Side

3"

Side   3"   Bottom   Fold   Side

Side

114   *You Can Be a Puppeteer!*

11*b* Box

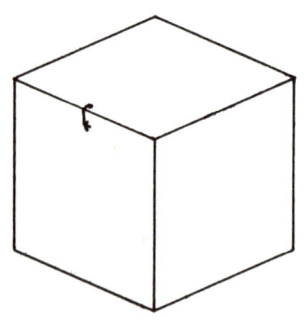

Fig. 11*c*. Stage for Scene Two

Fig. 11*d*. Hoe

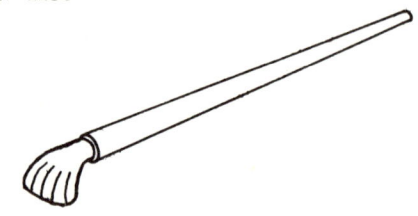

12

Dorcas Raised from the Dead

Puppet Play for two Performers

Directions

It would be well to record this play beforehand because of the five different voices required. When the play is recorded, the performers have only to manipulate the puppets. The recorder should either be hooked up to the church public address system, or put on a table away from the stage where it will not detract from the play. It should be in the front of the room or auditorium, so that the voices will sound as though they were coming from the stage, and one person should be designated to operate the machine.

CHARACTERS

Dorcas	
Stranger	first performer
Peter	
Esther	second performer
Miriam	

PROPS

Couch: This may be a small box, block of wood, or piece of foam rubber.

STACK OF CLOTHES, ROBES, AND BLANKETS: These should be pieces of cloth of various colors and textures, cut out to represent dresses, robes, blankets. They need not actually be finished products.

BOWL: This can be made out of clay or construction paper, or it could be a child's toy dish or a deep bottle cap.

WINDOW: (See instructions for WINDOW in chapter 7.)

DOOR: This is the opening in the curtain (see fig. 12a) for the puppets to enter and exit. It can be framed with paper or drawn or painted on the back curtain.

SIDE EXIT: Attach strip of curtain material (6"-8" wide) to top of backdrop. Extend to stage and attach, allowing end to fall below level of stage (see figs. 12a and 12b).

(SCENE ONE: *The interior of* DORCAS' *house, with* DORCAS *and* ESTHER *on stage.* DORCAS *has cloth in hand. As the curtain opens,* ESTHER *walks across stage and picks up one of the garments off of the pile of clothes.*)

ESTHER: Dorcas, you certainly have made a lot of clothes.

DORCAS: I've just finished another dress, Esther. This ought to fit the little crippled girl that we saw yesterday. I told her father to come and get it today.

ESTHER: Dorcas, you've been working so hard lately. Are you feeling well? Perhaps you are working too hard.

DORCAS: One can never work too hard for the Lord Jesus. But, it is true, I am not feeling very well. Oh, Esther, it would be nice if Peter could visit us here in Joppa. He's at Lydda, and I do hope that he can come and visit us. His visit would be such an encouragement. (*Pauses.*) Well, I must start another garment. (*Lays the dress down on the stack of clothes and picks up another piece of cloth.*)

ESTHER: Perhaps you ought to rest, Dorcas. You look very tired.

DORCAS: There is so much work to do. I am glad that I can

Dorcas Raised from the Dead 117

help others and tell them about the Lord Jesus (*Knocking heard.*) Someone is at the door. (*Moves toward door; staggers, puts hand to head.*) For a truth, I do not feel well.

ESTHER: I will answer the door. (*Moves toward door,* DORCAS *moves back toward pile of clothes.*) I will see who is there. (*Sticks head out of door.*)

STRANGER (*off stage*): Is this the house of Tabitha who is called Dorcas?

ESTHER: Yes, it is.

DORCAS: It is the father of the little girl. Bid him enter.

STRANGER (*enters; bows first to* DORCAS, *then to* ESTHER): Greetings, Dorcas.

DORCAS: I have made a dress for your daughter. (*Picks up dress.*)

STRANGER: You are very kind. Today I have been able to work, so I will also be able to take some food home to my wife and child.

DORCAS: I know that you have not been able to work because you have been sick too. So, I have made a pot of soup for you. Wait, I will get it. You must take it home. I will go and get it. (*Moves toward side of stage, walks slowly, hand to head.*)

STRANGER: You are very kind. I thank you.

DORCAS: I am glad to do this to help you in the name of Jesus. (*Staggers and "clings" to back curtain for support.*)

ESTHER: Wait, Dorcas. I will get it. Here, you sit down on the couch and rest. (DORCAS *moves to couch;* ESTHER *goes offstage through side exit.*)

DORCAS: I am glad that you could come today, friend.

STRANGER: I have been thinking about the words you told to us yesterday, about the one called Jesus. You said that He is the Son of God, the Messiah. You said He was crucified for our sins, and that He arose from the dead. These words—they are wonderful words.

DORCAS: It is true, He did arise from the dead. Because He arose from the dead, we do not have to fear death. He has paid for our sin. He came into the world, and lived here as a man, but He is the Son of God, the Messiah. He is the Saviour of the world, and He loves you, my friend.

(ESTHER *returns through side exit, with bowl in her hands, walks over to* STRANGER, *and hands it to him.*)

STRANGER: Thank you. Thank you very much. I would like to bring my wife and come to the next gathering of the people who follow this Jesus. These words are good words.

DORCAS: Good, we want you to know the Lord Jesus. Here is the dress for your little girl. (*Walks over to pile of clothes; picks up the dress she laid down at beginning of play; takes it to the man and lays it over his arms.*)

STRANGER: Thank you very much. I will leave you now. Thank you for the clothes for my daughter and for the soup.

DORCAS: Good-bye, and the Lord Jesus bless you.

ESTHER: God be with you.

STRANGER: Good-bye. (*Leaves through doorway.*)

(DORCAS *staggers toward couch.*)

ESTHER (*runs to* DORCAS' *side and puts her arm around her*): Dorcas, what is the matter? Dorcas! Dorcas!

DORCAS: My head—I—I feel so strange. I— (*Slumps over.*)

ESTHER (*holds her up and tries to carry her, fails, and lays her down on floor*): Oh, Dorcas! Dorcas, what is the matter? (*Fans* DORCAS *with hand; rushes over and gets blanket off of pile of clothes; lays it over* DORCAS.) Oh, Dorcas. What's the matter? Oh, I'd better go get someone to help. Dorcas, do speak to me. Dorcas! (*Leans over* DORCAS; *then hurries out of room.*)

(*Curtain closes.*)

(SCENE TWO: *After a short pause, curtains open on the same scene, with* DORCAS *lying on couch,* fig. 12c; ESTHER *and* MIRIAM *enter through door.*)

Dorcas Raised from the Dead

MIRIAM: Look at all the clothes she made. (*Goes to pile of clothes; begins to handle them.*)

ESTHER: Miriam, I just don't know what we are going to do without our Dorcas. She was always doing good works.

MIRIAM: We shall miss her. Even the beggars on the street stop me and say that they will miss our good friend Dorcas.

ESTHER: Everyone loved her. The father of the little crippled girl came to this house yesterday and Dorcas gave him food and clothes for the little girl. Oh, poor Dorcas! What shall we do without you? (*Begins to weep.*)

ESTHER: I have heard that someone has gone to Joppa to call Peter.

MIRIAM: Yes, we must have our friend Peter here. Oh, just the other day Dorcas was saying that she would like to see Peter— and now—now she is dead.

ESTHER: Peter will be able to comfort us when he comes.

MIRIAM: When is he coming? I hope it will be soon. (*Knocking heard.*) Someone's at the door. Oh, I hope it is Peter. (*Goes to door.*)

(PETER *enters.* MIRIAM *points to* DORCAS. PETER *shakes head sadly, then nods to* ESTHER.)

ESTHER (*bows to* PETER): Our dear friend Dorcas is dead, Peter.

PETER: So I have been told. I hurried from Joppa as soon as the news reached me.

MIRIAM: Look, Peter! Look at all the clothes Dorcas made for the poor.

ESTHER: She was so full of good works. (MIRIAM *and* ESTHER *move toward pile of garments; pick them up one by one, looking at them.*) See the blanket she made. And look at this cloth.

MIRIAM: Oh, Peter, we will miss her. She was always speaking to someone about the Lord Jesus.

ESTHER: Our poor Dorcas is dead! (*Begins to weep.*)

PETER: Leave me now. Leave me. Leave the room. I want to pray.

(ESTHER *and* MIRIAM *bow toward* PETER *and leave through side exit.*)

(PETER *kneels—to do this, fold his hands together in attitude of prayer, bend body forward, and bring your whole arm down a bit so that* PETER *seems to be kneeling; while he is praying he is not looking at or facing* DORCAS. *After a few seconds,* PETER *gets up, turns toward* DORCAS, *takes a couple of steps nearer the couch, and speaks—moves hand and points toward heaven*): Tabitha! Arise! (*Note: This must be spoken slowly and very clearly; for it should not be repeated, and you want to be sure that the audience understands* PETER's *words.*)

DORCAS (*sits up—to make this motion, bring your hand up, with the wrist still resting on the couch. She shakes her head, looks around the room, and then speaks*): Oh, Peter! Welcome, Peter, welcome. I am so happy to see you.

PETER (*walks toward side of stage where* MIRIAM *and* ESTHER *have just exited; sticks head behind curtain and calls*): Esther! Miriam! Come here! Come here!

(MIRIAM *and* ESTHER *enter. They look at* PETER, *who points toward* DORCAS. *They look at the couch; fall backward in surprise and gasp.*)

ESTHER: Oh! Oh!

MIRIAM: Dorcas?

(*They cling to each other for a moment in fright, then look at* PETER *and rush forward towards* DORCAS; *they kneel at the side of the couch.*)

MIRIAM: Dorcas! You are alive!

ESTHER: Dorcas! You are well. God has given you back to us! God has given you back to us. When the people hear about this wonderful thing that God has done, they will praise His name and believe that Jesus is truly the Son of God.

Dorcas Raised from the Dead

DORCAS: (*arising from couch*): Peter, I am so glad that you have come. You must be hungry. Let me get some soup for you.
(*Curtain closes.*)

122   *You Can Be a Puppeteer!*

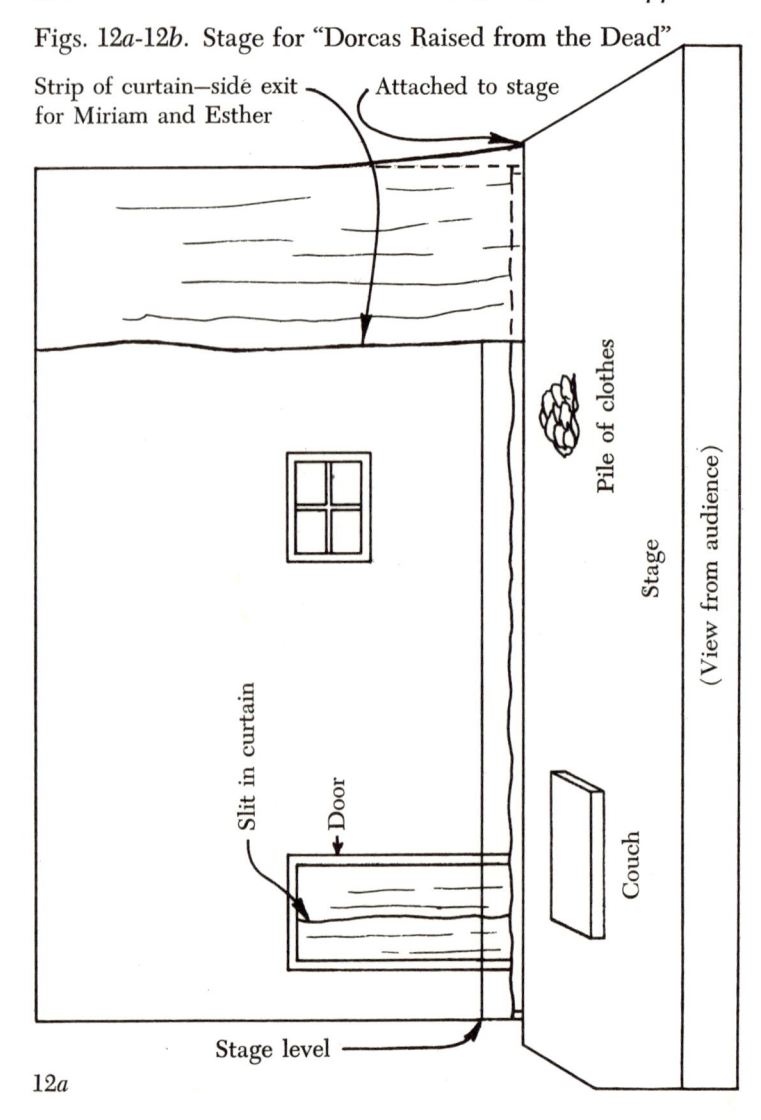

Figs. 12a-12b. Stage for "Dorcas Raised from the Dead"

Strip of curtain—side exit for Miriam and Esther

Attached to stage

Pile of clothes

Stage

(View from audience)

Slit in curtain

Door

Couch

Stage level

12a

Dorcas Raised from the Dead

123

12b

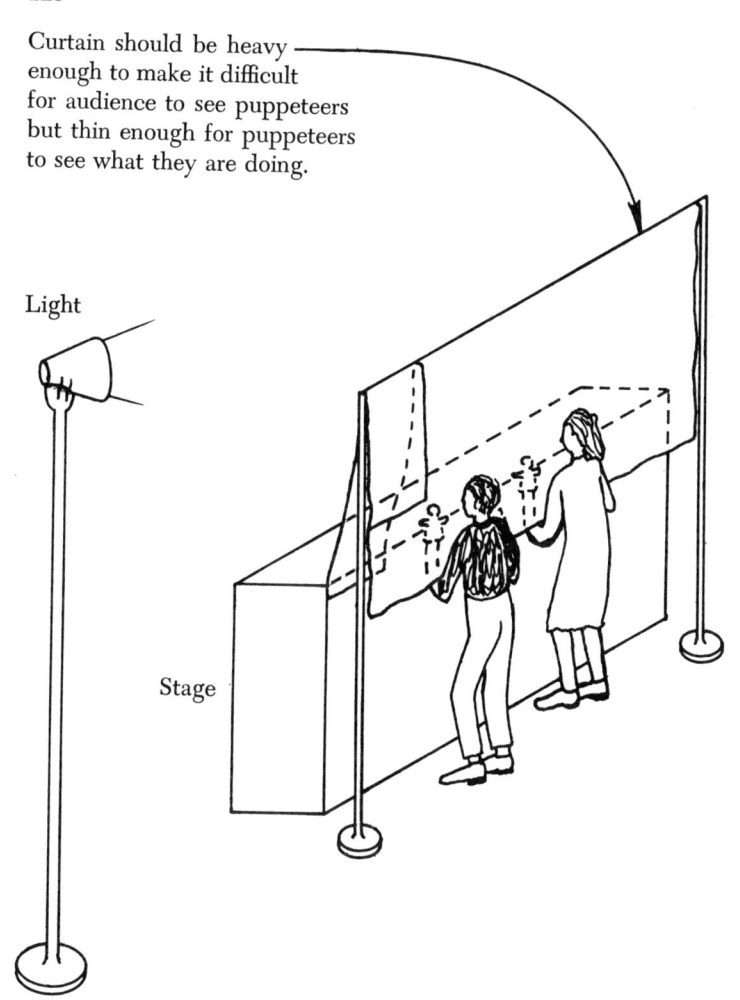

Curtain should be heavy enough to make it difficult for audience to see puppeteers but thin enough for puppeteers to see what they are doing.

Light

Stage

(Back and side view of stage)

124   *You Can Be a Puppeteer!*

Fig. 12c. Puppet on couch

Palm of hand up

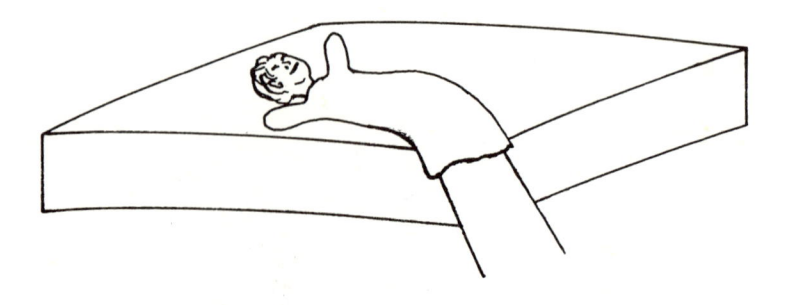